KNOW THYSELF

SOULFUL JOURNEY OF TODAY'S MAN

ARWIN VALENCIA, MD

Copyright Notice

Copyright © 2025 by ANG Power Publishing House.

All Rights Reserved.

No part of this publication, including but not limited to Know Thyself: Soulful Journey of Today's Man, may be reproduced, stored in a database or retrieval system, or distributed, or transmitted in any form or by any means, including photocopying, recording, or other electronic or mechanical methods, without the prior written permission of the copyright holder, except in the case of brief quotations embodied in critical reviews and certain other noncommercial uses permitted by copyright law. For permission requests, write to the copyright holder at the address below.

ANG POWER PUBLISHING HOUSE
PO BOX 10735 / Glendale, CA 91209-USA
ANGPowerPHouse@Gmail.com
ISBN: 978-1-966837-12-1

All trademarks, service marks, product names, and logos referenced in this book are the property of their respective owners. Know Thyself: Soulful Journey of Today's Man are the intellectual property of Dr. Arwin Valencia, MD and are protected under copyright law.

Disclaimer: The author and publisher have made every effort to ensure the accuracy of the information in this publication. However, they assume no responsibility for errors or omissions or for any consequences resulting from the use of the information provided. This book is intended for educational and informational purposes only and does not constitute professional or legal advice.

First Edition - Printed in the United States of America

TABLE OF CONTENTS

Introduction 1
Chapter 1 - Know Thyself: Awakening the Soul's Journey 5
Chapter 2 - Dissecting the Anatomy of the Soul 12
Chapter 3 - Energy: Currency of the Universe............................16
Chapter 4 - Vibration: The Language of the Universe 20
Chapter 5 - Morphic Field: Reservoir of All Knowing 24
Chapter 6 - Astrology: Unlocking the Cosmos............................28
Chapter 7 - Cosmic Lovers: Divine Masculine and Feminine 32
Chapter 8 - Gaia: Cradle of Our Awareness 36
Chapter 9 - As Above, So Below; As Within, So Without 40
Chapter 10 - Mysticism: Illuminating the Mind 44
Chapter 11 - When the Student Is Ready, the Teacher Will Appear. 48
Chapter 12 - Your Identity is Your Reality 52
Chapter 13 - Healing the Wounded Warrior 58
Chapter 14 - Ancestral Trauma, Karma, and Spiritual Coma 62
Chapter 15 - Shadow Work: Removing the Ego Mask.................66
Chapter 16 - Over-Analysis Leads to Paralysis 69
Chapter 17 - What We Resist, Persists..72
Chapter 18 - We Attract What We Are, Not What We Want 77
Chapter 19 - Be Still and Know That You Are God....................80
Chapter 20 - Life Happens For You, Not To You 84
Chapter 21 – Dis-ease/Disease: Symptoms of Spiritual Misalignment 87
Chapter 22 - Relationships: Our Spiritual Contracts 91
Chapter 23 - Kindred Spirits: Our Soulful Connections...............95
Chapter 24 - Spirit Guides: Our Divine Helpers 99
Chapter 25 - Breathwork: Our Connection to the Divine 103
Chapter 26 - Synchronicity: The Cosmic Nudge 106

Chapter 27 - Imagination: The Magic Wand of Creation 110
Chapter 28 - Dreams: Whispers from the Subconscious 114
Chapter 29 - Dark Night of the Soul: Bottomless Chasm 118
Chapter 30 - The Void: The In-Between of Desire and Manifestation 123
Chapter 31 - Gratitude: Gateway to Abundance.........................128
Chapter 32 - Compassion: Hallmark of the Integrated Soul 134
Chapter 33 - Transforming Love from Emotion to Foundation.140
Chapter 34 - Quantum Jumping Through the Matrix 145
Chapter 35 - Soul Trap and the Karmic Wheel 149
Chapter 36 - Patience: Waiting for Divine Timing....................156
Chapter 37 - Perspective, Perspective, Perspective 160
Chapter 38 - Be the Change You Wish to See in the World......170
Chapter 39 - See the Invisible: Believe in the Impossible 173
Chapter 40: Heart: The Center of Our Being............................177
Compassion: The Soul's Embrace..182
About the Author 185

To My Father... The True Mystic

"What You Seek Is Seeking You"

Rumi

What Happens

What happens when your soul
Begins to awaken
Your eyes
And your heart
And the cells of your body
To the great Journey of Love?
First there is wonderful laughter
And probably precious tears
And a hundred sweet promises
And those heroic vows
No one can ever keep.
But still God is delighted and amused
You once tried to be a saint.
What happens when your soul
Begins to awake in this world
To our deep need to love
And serve the Friend?
O the Beloved
Will send you
One of His wonderful, wild companions - Like Hafiz.

                                                       Hafez

Introduction

The journey through life has been a profound eye-opener for me. From early childhood, I began to question many things, particularly as someone who leaned more toward introspection than social interaction. Most of these inquiries had no direct or conclusive answers but instead invited exploration through philosophy and spirituality. Unfortunately, few in my sphere could provide satisfying or consistent insights, as they were often entangled in their own life dramas. Fortunately, my father, though busy as the family's provider, took the time to offer what answers he could. He, too, had a deep interest in spiritual matters.

I was raised in a devout Catholic environment, both culturally and through years of Catholic education. As I began to glimpse the mystery of my existence, more questions surfaced, and my curiosity deepened. For years, I explored various religions and philosophical traditions, but this quest had to pause when I shifted focus to a demanding medical career. Though pushed to the background, the longing never disappeared. No matter how much I tried to suppress it, it would resurface—calling for my attention.

Years of practicing as a physician caring for newborns, and later helping care for the elderly at the twilight of life, gave me unique insight into the entire spectrum of human existence—from its beginning to its end. These experiences rekindled my original yearning and, with more time and mental space, I returned to the inner quest for truth—not through outward validation, but inward exploration.

I feel fortunate to be alive during this era, with access to abundant resources: literature, digital media, social platforms, and spiritual communities. Through these avenues, I've connected with kindred spirits—soul groups, if you will—who are also on this path of awakening. Despite our diverse socioeconomic, cultural, and religious backgrounds, we share a deep commonality that transcends division.

I'm convinced that now is the opportune moment to awaken and embrace our true, authentic selves. The Aquarian age of spiritual enlightenment and empowerment is upon us.

This book is my offering—insights drawn from my personal and collective inquiries. Transitioning from technical writing to this style was initially challenging, but once I allowed the ideas to flow freely, I found deep joy in the process. What began as a vision for 15–20 short essays evolved into 40 chapters. Each chapter could easily stand alone as its own volume, yet the messages interweave in service of a larger truth. The lyrical, philosophical tone reflects my passion to express these inner revelations.

"Know Thyself: Soulful Journey of Today's Man" is a testament to my spiritual pilgrimage. It is a co-creative effort with my higher self and the spiritual companions I've encountered. My deepest hope is that these insights reach those navigating their own journeys. Though we may be at different stages, the resonance will find its way to those ready to receive.

These realizations came when I quieted the ego and attuned to the "still small voice" within. While I once expected a guru to appear—like Sri Yukteswar to Paramahansa Yogananda, or Obi-Wan Kenobi and Master Yoda to Luke Skywalker—my true teacher was the higher aspect of myself, accessed in moments of stillness and nature. Whether walking, gardening, or taking solitary drives, I found myself tuning in to deeper truths.

Though I meditate regularly, I still struggle with focus—perhaps due to my borderline ADD and type-A tendencies. Yet I continue to show up. As Lao Tzu or the

Buddha said, "When the student is ready, the teacher will appear."

I believe we all have the ability to tune into these higher truths. The universe is always broadcasting—we must simply choose to listen. Are we ready to tune in?

It is my sincere hope that this book not only reaches your hands or bookshelf but also touches your heart. May each word speak, vibrate, and resonate with the unique frequency of your soul.

Much love to you—and enjoy the journey!

Chapter 1

Know Thyself: Awakening the Soul's Journey

Beneath the noise, a whisper calls,
Beyond the mind, where silence falls.
Not in the world, but deep inside,
The soul begins its sacred ride.

A mirror held, not just to see—
But to recall what it means to be.
Each breath a step, each thought a key,
Unlocking truth eternally.

Awake, arise, the path is clear—
The one you seek is always near.
Know thyself, and you will find
The boundless soul behind the mind.

We are infinite souls navigating a finite human experience. We orient ourselves in form, defining our identities through family, society, and spiritual constructs shaped by the collective expectations of our time.

Many of us remain unaware of our true essence, mistaking ourselves for the body, the mind, or even the thoughts that drift through our awareness. Yet these are merely layers — programmed into us from birth — shaping our reality and keeping us bound to cycles of fear, desire, and survival. We spend much of our lives anchoring our identities to fleeting things: job titles, wealth, appearance, status, and relationships. But all these are temporary. The more tightly we cling to them, the more deeply we suffer when they inevitably change or fade. Such attachments perpetuate the illusion of separation — from others, from the Source, and even from our own true nature — though in truth, all is interconnected.

Can we truly know ourselves beyond the familiar identity that confines us in this illusion of reality? This false self makes us forget the imprint of our spiritual essence. The avatar of flesh and blood, meant only to serve as the vehicle for our journey of self-discovery, has become the entirety of our existence simply because we have identified with it so completely. Yet beneath these layers of confusion and conditioning lies something eternal and unchanging: the soul. The soul is the timeless observer, the quiet witness of all experience. But too often, it remains buried beneath layers of fear, distraction, and attachment.

The external world is neutral. It gains its flavor from our perception and interpretation. It mirrors our interactions back to us. The true battle is fought in the mind, where we often react impulsively instead of observing consciously. This world is a reflection of our inner landscape — our turmoil or our peace, our attachments or our freedom. Attachment feeds fear, which is the very antithesis of our essence as beings of pure, divine love. Fear begets illusions of lack, limitation, and separation.

Fear leads us to disempowering reactions, born from identification with the false self — a mere shadow of our authentic soul, shaped by external programming. It manifests in our cognitive dissonance, our narcissistic tendencies, and our endless hunger for material success, which never truly satisfies. Fear is the strongest force keeping us anchored to the lower frequencies of existence: fear of loss, fear of death, fear of not being enough. But when we face our fears with courage and awareness, we begin to dissolve the chains that bind us to this illusion.

The soul's journey is about returning to truth — remembering who we already are. It is not about becoming something new, but rather unbecoming everything we are not. This is the heart of shadow work: dismantling the reptilian mind's framework of survival, rooted in fight-or-flight instincts and the false perception of separation. In truth, we are integrated beings, unified across the spectrum of lower and higher selves, individual yet fractal reflections of the Divine. Each fractal is a complete hologram of the whole. Shadow work also involves reclaiming the hidden parts of ourselves — those we have denied or suppressed. When we bring light to these shadows, we reclaim our power and move closer to wholeness.

Meditation and mindfulness are keys that unlock the door to our true nature. They quiet the noise of the world and the chatter within, allowing us to hear the gentle whispers of the soul. Some seekers turn to plant medicines, energy healing, or sacred geometry. These tools can act as catalysts, opening portals to higher states of consciousness and offering glimpses of the web that connects all life. But they are guides, not destinations. The true journey lies within, in the integration of these insights into everyday life.

At its pinnacle, this journey leads us to Samadhi — a profound state of unity consciousness, where the illusion of separation dissolves entirely. In this state, we realize we are not apart from God but expressions of the Divine itself. This is the awakening of the Christ consciousness, the recognition that the kingdom of heaven resides within us.

I firmly believe that, as fractal expressions of Source, we are already whole and lack nothing. Creation itself is the Creator's way of experiencing infinite expressions of individuality. To do this, it projects itself into the illusion of limitation — explaining the constructs of time and space, which allow us to navigate existence. To fully experience this, a receiver is required to embody the smaller aspect of the whole: this is the role of the human avatar, the lower self. The ego serves as the mechanism that keeps us tethered to this game, helping us manage survival in this unfamiliar realm of duality.

The principle is simple, though we often become lost in the complexity of the 3D experience. Life's emotional highs and lows entangle us, and we begin to identify with our perceived limitations, forgetting our true nature. We become ensnared in the cycle of karma instead of transcending it, trapped in its vortex like the ouroboros, endlessly devouring its own tail.

Yet despite the appearance of limitation, the drive to create still burns within us — for creation is our very nature as embodied fragments of the Creator. This reflects the Hermetic principle of correspondence: "As above, so below; as within, so without." When we fully embrace this truth, we understand that life is not something happening to us but the authentic experience of who we are! What we perceive externally is simply a reflection of our internal vibrational state. The battle is vibrational in nature, and it comes down to a simple choice: alignment with our divine self or continued entrapment in the illusion of the lower self.

From this perspective, we see that life is not passive. It is an active, participatory experience — one that we create and direct. Life becomes the canvas for our soul's expression, shaped by the frequency we embody.

With Source as the projector (Divine Masculine) and ourselves as the receiver (Divine Feminine), we complete the sacred equation of creation. From no-thing, we birth new realities into form, stepping out of victimhood and into victory.

We are both the student and the teacher, the dreamer and the dream. Source projects; we receive. Our purpose is to remember, to awaken, and to create from this place of knowing. When we align with our soul's purpose, life flows with grace and meaning. We cease resisting what is and begin to dance with the rhythm of existence.

The destination of this journey — our hero's quest — is the awakening of the soul: to find and truly know thyself amid the chaos and limitations of this world. This is the ultimate alchemy. Through our trials and triumphs, we transmute the base metals of fear and ignorance into the gold of wisdom and love. This is the true philosopher's stone: the transformation of self.

Know thyself. This is the first step and the final destination. The journey is inward, and the treasure we seek has always been within us.

Chapter 2

Dissecting the Anatomy of the Soul

Beneath the veil of flesh and bone,
A silent truth is carved in stone.
Not sinew, blood, or breath define—
But light, and echo, and the divine.

A thought, a wound, a whispered prayer,
Each fiber shaped from love laid bare.
The soul's not found in form or chart,
But etched in silence, flame, and heart.

We peel the layers, seek control,
Yet lose the map to make it whole.
For soul is song, not part, but whole—
A sacred dance, a living scroll.

The soul is widely regarded as the immaterial, non-physical essence of a human being—what gives life to the body, animates consciousness, and defines individuality. It is seen as the core of one's being, the element that embodies thoughts, emotions, desires, and a unique identity. Across religious, philosophical, and spiritual traditions, the soul has been the subject of profound inquiry, each perspective offering its own understanding of the soul's origin, nature, and destiny.

Interpretations of the soul vary significantly. Some traditions view it as the seat of emotion, thought, and moral conscience. Others regard it as the spiritual aspect that connects the individual to the divine. In many belief systems, the soul is not static; it evolves, grows, and continues its journey beyond physical death.

Religious and philosophical systems present diverse and often contrasting explanations. In Christianity, the soul is the eternal essence created by God, destined to outlive the body. In Buddhism, however, there is no enduring soul; instead, the focus is on the impermanence and interdependence of all things. Hinduism posits that the soul, or *Atman*, is an unchanging, eternal self that is ultimately one with *Brahman*, the universal spirit. Judaism conceptualizes the *Neshamah* as the divine breath that animates the body, while in Islam, the *Ruh* is a divine creation that exists in tandem with the physical body.

In some traditions, the soul and spirit are seen as distinct but interrelated. The soul is often considered the life force or emotional-mental center of the individual, while the spirit is associated with divine consciousness and purpose. Though these terms are frequently used interchangeably, they reflect nuanced dimensions of human existence: the inner landscape of experience and the transcendent connection to a higher reality.

Various schools of thought have also proposed that the soul is not a singular entity but comprises multiple facets. Plato famously divided the soul into three parts—reason, spirit, and appetite—each governing a different aspect of human behavior. Some Christian frameworks view the soul as composed of mind, will, and emotion, with the intellect often leading the other components. Ancient Egyptian belief identified several soul elements: the *Ba* (personality), *Ka* (vital essence), and *Ib* (heart). Aristotle categorized souls according to life forms—plants with nutritive souls, animals with sensitive souls, and humans with rational souls.

The concept of a "higher self" adds another layer to this inquiry. In many spiritual and philosophical traditions, it represents a more evolved, divine aspect of the self—one that transcends ego and connects us with our true purpose. In Hinduism, this is closely related to *Atman*. In some modern spiritualities, the higher self is tied to the idea of the *Oversoul*, a collective spiritual consciousness that unites all individual souls. This aligns with the Hindu notion of *Paramatman*, the supreme soul or absolute reality.

Philosophically, thinkers like Gottfried Wilhelm Leibniz introduced metaphysical constructs such as the monad—an indivisible, soul-like unit of consciousness. He proposed that reality is composed not of material atoms but of spiritual substances, each reflecting the universe in its own unique way. These monads, harmonized by divine order, echo the belief that each soul contains a microcosm of the cosmos.

In conclusion, the soul is far more than a metaphysical abstraction—it is the living architecture of human experience, consciousness, and purpose. Across centuries and civilizations, it has been dissected into components, unified in essence, and exalted as the bridge between the human and the divine. To **dissect the anatomy of the soul** is to explore not only what makes us alive, but what makes us eternal. It is a journey into the unseen dimensions of our being, revealing the profound truth that we are more than bodies—we are soul in motion, reaching ever closer to our highest form.

Chapter 3

Energy: Currency of the Universe

Invisible tide, forever in flow,
From stars above to roots below.
Not bought or sold, yet all things trade,
In light and thought, in spark and shade.

A silent pulse, a sacred stream,
That powers life and fuels the dream.
Give with love, receive with grace—
This sacred currency shapes time and space.

Energy, at its core, is defined as the ability to perform work. In physics, it is recognized as a fundamental quantity that exists in multiple forms—potential, kinetic, thermal, light, sound, and electricity. It can be stored or set in motion, but according to the law of conservation, energy cannot be created or destroyed—only transformed.

Matter and energy are the two foundational components of the Universe. Yet, much of what constitutes the cosmos remains a mystery. Scientists grapple with the fact that the majority of matter is invisible and the source of most energy remains unknown. Remarkably, about 68% of the universe's energy content is attributed to a force known as **dark energy**—a mysterious phenomenon believed to drive the universe's accelerated expansion. Dark matter and ordinary matter comprise the remaining 32%, with only a small fraction consisting of visible energy in the form of electromagnetic radiation.

This visible energy, spanning from radio waves to gamma rays, is primarily transported by photons—particles of light that travel immense distances, carrying with them information about the structure and events of the cosmos. The sun, through the immense power of nuclear fusion, acts as the principal energy source for life on Earth. This stellar energy is harnessed in various ways—fossil fuels, nuclear power, and renewable sources—all extensions of the original cosmic fire.

At the quantum level, the boundaries between matter and energy blur. In this strange subatomic realm, particles behave both like matter and waves, and energy exists in discrete packets called quanta. This reality challenges the classical worldview, revealing a dynamic, interconnected field where matter and energy are simply different expressions of the same unified essence.

Beyond the scientific, energy also serves as a profound metaphor for human experience. Energy is the universal currency—not just in the physical sense, but emotionally, mentally, and spiritually. Our thoughts, emotions, and actions are expressions of energy. Just as money facilitates transactions in society, energy fuels interactions in the Universe.

When we direct our focus—our attention—we are investing our energy. This investment shapes our experiences. Focus on negativity, and more negativity tends to follow; focus on positivity, and we often find life echoing that vibration. As beings formed from stardust, we are intrinsically connected to the energy of the cosmos. What we emit energetically—through thought, word, and deed—ripples outward and shapes what returns to us.

This awareness calls for a mindful, intentional way of living. By understanding that energy is both the mechanism and medium of existence, we are invited to live with greater consciousness and responsibility. Where we place our energy becomes a sacred act, an offering to the unfolding of our lives.

Energy is not merely a force to be measured; it is the pulse of life itself. It is the language through which the universe speaks, evolves, and remembers. To realize that energy is the true currency of existence is to awaken to our power as co-creators. In every thought we think, in every action we take, we are spending this currency—either enriching or impoverishing the reality we inhabit. When we honor the sacredness of energy, we begin to live in harmony with the Universe, recognizing that every exchange is a reflection of what we value most. In this awareness, we do not merely exist—we begin to truly *participate* in the divine economy of creation.

Chapter 4

Vibration: The Language of the Universe

By motion's thread, all form is spun,
From atom's hum to star and sun.
In silence speaks the pulse of force,
A rhythm charting nature's course.

Each sound, each light, a coded sign,
A wave that maps the grand design.
Not words, but frequency aligns
The mind to realms beyond confined.

In every beat, a truth concealed—
The universe in tone revealed.

We live in a universe where the governing force is energy and vibration. Energy is the capacity to do work, while vibration is the rhythmic motion of energy expressed through oscillation. Vibration is not merely a movement—it is the way energy manifests and transfers, serving as the invisible thread that weaves the fabric of existence.

In the realm of quantum physics, the universe is understood as a vast field of vibrating energy. At atomic and subatomic levels, everything is in constant motion. Even objects that appear still are alive with microscopic vibration. This motion is not just mechanical—it is foundational, giving rise to all forms of matter and experience. Different frequencies and patterns of vibration result in the diverse expressions of energy, from particles and forces to emotions and thoughts.

Frequency is what defines the nature of a vibration. Each frequency corresponds to a particular type of energy or phenomenon. From a quantum perspective, reality is a boundless field of potential energy, unstable until directed by awareness. Our consciousness plays a vital role in shaping this energy. Each person emits a unique vibrational frequency, determined by their level of awareness and inner state, and this determines the quality of their experiences.

To say that vibration is the "language of the universe" is to suggest that all life communicates through energy frequencies. This concept, rooted in both ancient spiritual traditions and modern science, reveals that by aligning with these vibrations, we can deepen our understanding of the universe and our place within it.

This language is not spoken—it is felt. It manifests through intuition, emotion, symbolism, dreams, and physical sensation. When we raise our vibration through practices like meditation, gratitude, clean living, and positive thought, we begin to attune ourselves to higher frequencies. These frequencies are linked to clarity, healing, love, and spiritual insight.

The Law of Attraction, for instance, teaches that our thoughts and emotions—vibrational by nature—magnetize experiences of similar frequency into our lives. This is why affirmations and prayers stated in the present tense are powerful; they harmonize with the universe's understanding of time as the eternal now.

Even scientific theories support this vibrational reality. String theory, a modern framework in theoretical physics, posits that the fundamental building blocks of the universe are vibrating strings of energy. Human beings, too, have measurable resonant frequencies. Research has shown that the human body, mind, and even cells operate at specific vibrational levels.

Among the many tools available for tuning into these frequencies, Solfeggio frequencies stand out. Originally a method for sight-singing in music education, they are now believed to hold healing and transformative properties. For example, 639 Hz enhances compassion and connection, while 852 Hz supports clarity, intuition, and awakening. These frequencies act as keys, unlocking access to higher dimensions of thought and being.

In understanding these principles, we now realize that this universe is composed not of things but of energies, not of silence but of vibration, we are not separate from the cosmic song—we are instruments within it. The more we awaken to this truth, the more we begin to live in harmony with the sacred rhythm of all existence. To speak the language of the universe is to remember that we are not only receivers of energy—we are also transmitters, capable of tuning our frequency to love, healing, and higher wisdom. When we raise our vibration, we do not just change our lives—we become co-creators in the unfolding of the cosmos.

Chapter 5

Morphic Field: Reservoir of All Knowing

In silence it speaks, unseen yet near,
A field of wisdom beyond what's clear.
Echoes of thought, of form, of flame,
Patterns repeating, never the same.

The past informs the now to grow,
A wave of memory's endless flow.
Not bound by time, nor space confined,
A cosmic net of the collective mind.

Tap the field, the truth shall rise—
The soul remembers, the spirit flies.

The concept of the **morphic field**, introduced by biologist Rupert Sheldrake, proposes that all living beings—and even non-living forms—exist within fields of evolutionary information that shape their form, behavior, and development. Unlike physical fields such as electromagnetism, morphic fields are non-material patterns that act as invisible blueprints, guiding biological and behavioral evolution across time.

Sheldrake's theory, known as the *hypothesis of formative causation*, suggests that these fields are influenced by the accumulated experiences of similar organisms. Through a process called **morphic resonance**, past patterns of activity influence present behavior, making certain outcomes increasingly likely the more they occur. In essence, the more a particular behavior or form is repeated, the easier it becomes for it to reoccur—across individuals and generations. This idea mirrors psychological concepts like Carl Jung's *collective unconscious* and aligns with non-local dynamics observed in quantum physics.

Morphic fields are believed to exist for all forms of life, influencing everything from cellular development to mental activity, social behavior, and learned responses. For example, experiments have shown that rats trained to navigate a maze can indirectly help rats of the same species—across the globe—learn the same maze faster. This implies the presence of a shared informational field accessible beyond direct contact or communication. These fields are further categorized into mental, behavioral, and social fields, each guiding different aspects of existence.

On a quantum level, morphic fields are thought to function through a kind of "action at a distance," a non-local mechanism in which information is transmitted instantaneously across space. This parallels the behavior of quantum entanglement and suggests that morphic fields could be analogous to quantum fields—fundamental structures that permeate the universe and give rise to matter and experience.

More than a scientific hypothesis, the morphic field can be viewed as a **collective memory system**—a reservoir of knowledge, behaviors, and archetypes that influence not just individuals, but entire species. This theory also underpins social coordination in animal groups, such as flocks of birds or schools of fish, and finds resonance in therapeutic models like *family constellations*, which explore inherited emotional patterns.

To call the morphic field a **"reservoir of all knowing"** is to recognize it as a vast, interconnected matrix of information—one that holds the memory of all that has been, and guides the emergence of what is yet to come. As individualized expressions of the divine, we are not separate from this field but are active participants within it. Through conscious awareness and intention, we tap into this infinite matrix, not only receiving its patterns but also imprinting our own. In this way, we become not just recipients of information, but creators—programming our reality with each thought, word, and action.

The morphic field invites us to awaken to our role as co-creators in a living universe—one where the past, present, and future are unified by patterns of knowing, and where each soul is empowered to shape the unfolding of collective consciousness.

Chapter 6

Astrology: Unlocking the Cosmos

The stars align, a silent guide,
Their ancient whispers never hide.
In cosmic dance, the truth is spun,
As moon and planets shape each one.
A map above, a mirror below—
Unlock the path your soul must know.

Astrology is the ancient study of how the movements and positions of celestial bodies—such as the sun, moon, and planets—are believed to influence human behavior and world events. At its core, astrology suggests a connection between the cosmos and human existence, asserting that celestial patterns hold symbolic meaning that can provide insight into personality, potential, and life circumstances.

The foundational tool of astrology is the birth chart, or horoscope, which maps the positions of the planets at the time of a person's birth. This chart is interpreted through the twelve zodiac signs and twelve houses, each governing different aspects of life—from identity and emotions to relationships and career. Beyond the individual, mundane astrology looks at broader planetary alignments to understand political shifts, social trends, and global events.

Historically, astrology was not just a tool for personal guidance but a revered practice embedded in culture and governance. Ancient civilizations like the Babylonians believed celestial phenomena were messages from the gods, revealing divine will and shaping destinies. The Romans saw eclipses and comets as omens, while Greek thinkers such as Aristotle envisioned a universe in which the celestial and terrestrial realms were intrinsically connected. Astrology influenced not only spiritual practices but also the timing of rituals, agricultural activities, and political decisions.

Astrology has also long shared a space with mysticism. For many spiritual seekers, it serves as a bridge between the material and the metaphysical, offering a symbolic language to interpret the unseen forces that shape human experience. Mystics often view astrology as a roadmap to align with universal energies and to better understand one's soul journey.

Despite its deep roots and widespread appeal, astrology remains outside the realm of mainstream science. Modern scientific inquiry has found no empirical evidence that celestial bodies exert any measurable influence on human behavior or fate. Attempts to link astrology with quantum physics often misuse or misinterpret scientific terminology, leading to skepticism among scientists. Quantum physics explores the laws governing subatomic particles, while astrology operates on symbolic interpretation rather than measurable causation.

Still, for many, astrology offers more than prediction—it provides reflection. It serves as a framework for self-awareness, helping individuals explore their patterns, challenges, and strengths. In an increasingly complex world, astrology presents a way to find meaning in chaos, to feel connected to something greater, and to navigate life with a sense of cosmic rhythm.

While astrology may not meet the standards of scientific validation, its enduring presence throughout human history speaks to its psychological, cultural, and spiritual relevance. It offers a symbolic map for understanding the inner and outer worlds, guiding individuals through cycles of growth, transformation, and purpose. Whether seen as divine insight, ancient wisdom, or a mirror for introspection, astrology continues to unlock the cosmos—not by predicting fate with certainty, but by inspiring people to reflect on their place in the universe and the mysteries that lie beyond.

Chapter 7

Cosmic Lovers: Divine Masculine and Feminine

In stardust breath and sacred flame,
Two forces dance without a name.
He is structure, bold and bright,
She is mystery, flowing light.

He stands firm, a mountain's grace,
She moves like moonlight's soft embrace.
Together born from Source above,
They shape the world through boundless love.

No chase, no chain—just pure becoming,
In silence deep, their hearts are humming.
A cosmic pulse, both fierce and tender—
The sacred union: soul's surrender.

The universe operates through a dance of dualities. From the macrocosm of galaxies to the microcosm of human experience, everything exists in pairs—complementary forces that shape reality. This principle is echoed in disciplines as diverse as physics, philosophy, and mysticism, symbolized beautifully by archetypes like yin and yang. Among the most profound of these dualities are the Divine Masculine and Divine Feminine—two sacred energies that, when balanced, guide the soul toward wholeness.

The Divine Masculine: Structure and Manifestation

The Divine Masculine represents the archetypal qualities of action, clarity, structure, and conscious will. Spiritually, it is the transmitting force—the focused energy that sets intentions into motion and brings ideas into tangible form. While it is often associated with traits such as leadership, logic, courage, and integrity, its awakened form also includes empathy, protection, and a deep sense of responsibility. It is not rigid masculinity rooted in domination, but a divine expression that holds space, initiates, and provides a stable ground upon which life can flourish.

The Divine Feminine: Intuition and Creation

The Divine Feminine is the receptive, nurturing, and life-giving energy that flows through all creation. It is the intuitive, emotional, and interconnected force that nourishes the inner and outer worlds. Associated with qualities such as compassion, creativity, patience, and inner knowing, the feminine embodies the sacred mystery of becoming. Far from being passive, this energy is dynamic in its ability to heal, transform, and give birth to new realities. It calls individuals to slow down, listen deeply, and align with the rhythms of the soul and nature.

Sacred Parallels Across Traditions

Many spiritual traditions have expressed this duality through myth, theology, and cosmology. In Hinduism, Shiva and Shakti represent consciousness and dynamic energy respectively—together symbolizing the inseparability of stillness and movement. In Christianity, while not explicitly framed in the same terms, the idea of God as both Father and the nurturing presence of the Holy Spirit echoes the balance of masculine and feminine aspects within the divine mystery. These traditions remind us that sacred union is a universal theme.

Wholeness Through Integration

The journey toward inner harmony involves recognizing, honoring, and integrating both masculine and feminine energies within oneself. These energies are not tied to gender but exist as potentials in every being. When either is overexpressed or suppressed, imbalance arises—manifesting as personal discontent or relational conflict. But when they dance in unison, they cultivate inner alignment, emotional intelligence, creative expression, and empowered action.

Balancing these energies deepens one's connection to self, enhances relationships, and promotes trust in the natural unfolding of life. The Divine Masculine builds the container; the Divine Feminine fills it with meaning. One provides direction, the other nurtures depth. Together, they move the soul from resistance to surrender, from fear to love.

Conclusion: The Cosmic Union

At the heart of the cosmos lies the sacred marriage of the Divine Masculine and Feminine—eternal lovers whose union births universes. This divine interplay reflects not only a metaphysical principle but a spiritual calling: to embody balance, to honor both structure and flow, logic and intuition, action and receptivity. When we awaken these archetypal energies within, we step into our fullest potential—not as fractured beings seeking completion, but as whole souls radiating harmony.

In embracing the cosmic lovers within, we transcend separation and align with the deeper rhythm of creation. For in their embrace, we discover the path to unity, healing, and divine remembrance.

Chapter 8

Gaia: Cradle of Our Awareness

Gaia, cradle of our soul,
In her embrace, we are made whole.
Beneath the stars, beneath the sky,
Her whispers echo, never shy.

Roots entwined, the earth's deep song,
In her arms, we all belong.
From mountains tall to oceans wide,
Gaia holds us, as we glide.

Awakening hearts, we come to see,
We are her children, wild and free.
Through every breath, in every sound,
Gaia's love is all around.

While there is no direct scientific proof that Earth itself possesses consciousness, a growing body of philosophical and speculative thought suggests that consciousness might be more fundamental to the universe than previously assumed. Concepts like "quantum consciousness" — though not empirically validated —

raise compelling questions about the nature and scope of awareness in the cosmos.

Ancient cultures across the globe embraced the idea of a living Earth, often personified as *Gaia* or the Earth Mother. These beliefs, rooted in animism, regarded all elements of nature as imbued with spirit or life force. Humanity was not seen as separate from the Earth, but as an expression of her consciousness — an interconnected part of a greater whole.

Modern science does not currently recognize nature as conscious in the same way humans are. However, the boundaries of this understanding are being tested. The Cambridge Declaration on Consciousness affirms that many animals — including mammals, birds, and octopuses — have the neurological substrates to support conscious experience. Even in the plant kingdom, researchers observe complex behaviors: plants can sense and respond to light, gravity, touch, and even neighboring organisms. Though lacking a brain, their sophisticated signaling systems invite philosophical reflection on what constitutes awareness.

Some theorists go further, proposing that consciousness is a fundamental force, akin to gravity or electromagnetism — not merely an emergent property of biological complexity. If consciousness permeates reality at a quantum level, through phenomena like entanglement and superposition, then its reach could extend far beyond the human mind, implying a non-local, interconnected field of awareness that underlies existence itself.

The challenge in defining consciousness lies in its inherently subjective nature. It involves perception, experience, and a sense of being — qualities not easily quantified. Yet, in the absence of a definitive model, the possibility that consciousness is distributed throughout nature — in varying degrees and forms — remains open for exploration.

From an esoteric perspective, Gaia is more than metaphor; she represents a planetary consciousness, a living, breathing organism with which humanity shares an energetic and spiritual bond. This worldview sees human consciousness as woven into the Earth's own awareness — rising and evolving together. The increasing recognition of this bond is not just spiritual idealism, but a call to reawaken our relationship with the Earth.

The *Schumann Resonance*, a set of electromagnetic frequencies resonating between Earth's surface and the ionosphere — particularly the 7.83 Hz frequency, sometimes called the Earth's "heartbeat" — has been linked in speculative research to human brainwave states and well-being. Though not conclusively proven, the idea that we are biologically attuned to Earth's natural rhythms reinforces the vision of a shared consciousness between planet and people.

The concept of Earth's "ascension" to the 5th dimension (5D) is a spiritual framework describing a collective elevation of awareness. While not grounded in empirical science, it reflects a transformative shift: from separation to unity, fear to love, and ego to higher purpose. This "New Earth" is imagined not as a place, but as a state of consciousness where harmony and interconnectedness prevail.

Ultimately, whether Earth's consciousness is an innate force or a projection of humanity's evolving awareness, the emerging paradigm is clear: we are not separate from the Earth, but participants in a greater field of intelligence. Gaia, as the cradle of our awareness, challenges us to remember that our well-being and evolution are deeply entwined with that of the planet. The more we awaken to this truth, the more we align with a conscious Earth — and a conscious future.

Chapter 9

As Above, So Below; As Within, So Without

The stars above reflect our soul,
A mirrored dance, a cosmic goal.
What stirs within, shall bloom without,
A silent truth beyond all doubt.

The sky and soil, the heart and mind,
Are threads of one great weave combined.
To shift the world, begin inside—
For all is one, no need to hide.

The phrase *"As above, so below; as within, so without"* is a profound philosophical principle suggesting that there is a mirroring or correspondence between the macrocosm—the universe—and the microcosm—the individual. Rooted in Hermeticism, this ancient teaching emphasizes the idea that what happens on one level of reality also reflects on another. It draws a bridge between the outer and inner worlds, the physical and metaphysical, the divine and the human.

The first part, *"As above, so below,"* points to the belief that the universal laws governing the cosmos also operate on Earth. Patterns observed in the stars, planets, and galaxies are echoed in the rhythms and structures of our planet. Seasonal cycles, tides, and natural laws are seen as expressions of celestial order.

The second part, *"As within, so without,"* invites us to look inward. It asserts that the thoughts, emotions, and beliefs we hold within shape our external experiences. Our reality becomes a reflection of our inner landscape. This interpretation is often embraced in spiritual traditions that highlight the power of self-awareness, suggesting that by transforming the self, we influence the world around us.

This principle of correspondence is echoed in the *Law of One*, the channeled teachings of Ra—an ancient purported consciousness—that describe all existence as fundamentally unified. According to this view, all distinctions are illusions of perspective, and everything is ultimately a manifestation of the same energy or consciousness, differentiated only by levels of awareness.

Scientific analogies can also help illustrate this concept. In **cosmology**, the same physical laws govern both galaxies and subatomic particles. In **mathematics**, fractals exhibit self-similarity—where smaller parts resemble the larger whole—revealing repeating patterns at every scale of existence. These scientific perspectives reinforce the idea that there is a structural and energetic continuity throughout the universe.

The alchemical interpretation of this principle ties spiritual transformation with material processes. In this context, personal evolution and enlightenment mirror the refinement and transmutation of elements—symbolizing the integration of spiritual truth with earthly existence.

Ultimately, this principle challenges the illusion of separation. It invites us to question whether the divide between the observer and the observed, the divine and the human, the cosmos and the self, is real—or whether it is merely a shift in perspective. When we look through a unified lens, we see that the same truth reverberates across all levels of being.

"As above, so below; as within, so without" is more than a mystical aphorism—it is an invitation to recognize the unity that underlies all things. Whether explored through spirituality, science, or introspection, it reminds us that the universe is not separate from us but expressed through us. In understanding this mirroring, we reclaim our role as co-creators, bridging the inner and outer

worlds, and awakening to the deeper order that connects all existence.

Chapter 10

Mysticism: Illuminating the Mind

Beyond the veil of thought and time,
The soul ascends in truths sublime.
In silent stillness, light is found,
Where sacred whispers soft resound.

No need for words, no need for sight,
The heart perceives the Infinite Light.
In union deep, the self unwinds—
Mysticism: it frees the mind.

Mysticism is the pursuit of direct, experiential knowledge of God, spiritual truth, or ultimate reality. It transcends intellectual reasoning, entering the sacred domain of intuition, insight, and inner knowing. At its heart, mysticism is not about doctrine or dogma, but about communion—a personal encounter with the divine that eludes ordinary language and defies conventional understanding.

Rooted in experiential awareness, mysticism offers a unique pathway to truth—one that moves beyond the limitations of the rational mind. The mystic seeks not just to understand the divine, but to merge with it, to dissolve the illusion of separation and experience a state of unity and wholeness. Across traditions, this mystical journey is characterized by practices such as prayer, meditation, contemplation, fasting, and silence, all aimed at expanding consciousness and deepening spiritual awareness.

In Christianity, mystics like Teresa of Ávila and John of the Cross described moments of ecstatic union with God, often marked by overwhelming peace, love, and light. In Eastern traditions, enlightenment is the awakening to the oneness of all existence—achieved through yoga, meditation, and mindfulness. In Sufism, the mystic path is a passionate longing for divine love, expressed through poetry, music, and remembrance (dhikr). Despite differing expressions, the essence remains the same: direct experience of the divine.

In our modern world—riddled with anxiety, disconnection, and existential crisis—mysticism offers a vital remedy. It restores our inner compass and invites us to rediscover the sacred dimension of life. Embracing mysticism doesn't mean abandoning logic; rather, it complements our intellect with contemplative wisdom.

This fusion of rational and mystical awareness allows us to perceive more wholly, love more deeply, and respond to life with compassion and creativity.

Mysticism teaches us that we are not merely observers of the divine, but participants in it. The yearning we feel—the deep, aching longing for something greater—is the soul's call to return to its Source. It is not a flaw in our humanity, but a reflection of our divine origin. From a Christian perspective, this longing is fulfilled in relationship with God through Christ, who promises "living water" to all who thirst—a symbol of the indwelling Spirit that nourishes and completes the soul.

In esoteric traditions, this same longing is seen as the awakening of the divine spark within—the Christ Consciousness, the rise of Kundalini, the Persian *Yar*, meaning "companion." Each metaphor points to the sacred union of the lover and the beloved within: the integration of spirit and self, masculine and feminine, heaven and earth. It is a reunion not only with God but with our deepest essence.

Mysticism: Illuminating the Mind is ultimately an invitation—to journey inward, to awaken the divine within, and to experience life not merely through intellect but through the sacred lens of unity and presence. In a fractured world, mysticism rekindles our connection to the eternal, reminding us that beyond the veil of separation lies an infinite well of love, peace, and truth. As we heed the soul's longing and embrace both head and heart, we begin to see with new eyes, guided not just by knowledge, but by illumination.

Chapter 11

When the Student Is Ready, the Teacher Will Appear

In silence deep, when hearts grow still,
And minds surrender stubborn will,
The veil is thin, the path is clear—
The teacher's voice draws ever near.

Not in books or halls of stone,
But in the truths we call our own,
A glance, a word, a sudden light—
The guide arrives in quiet night.

No step is lost, no lesson vain,
Each tear, each joy, each spark of pain,
Prepares the soul to truly see—
The teacher lives in you and me.

When we embark on a journey of awakening, we begin to question life—not just how it unfolds around us, but how it connects deeply to who we are. These are not questions with quick, definitive answers; they are questions of meaning and purpose, pointing us toward a greater understanding of ourselves and our place in the world. In seeking answers, we turn to books, spiritual teachers, psychologists, faith leaders, and various forms of guidance. Yet, more often than not, we struggle to find the perfect alignment between teacher and student.

This misalignment can be disheartening. It may tempt us to abandon the path altogether, retreating into old habits and familiar beliefs. Or it may inspire perseverance—to keep searching, to keep refining our discernment, and to trust the wisdom we already carry, putting it into practice as best we can.

Finding a spiritual guide requires introspection, patience, and an open heart. We must begin by understanding what we seek, what resonates with us, and what kind of teacher aligns with our values and aspirations. In doing so, we engage with communities, observe teachings, and stay attuned to what speaks to our inner truth.

Yet, the essential truth is often overlooked: this journey is not merely outward—it is a quest within. We are Divine beings experiencing the illusion of limitation. While traditional cultures may encourage seeking wisdom from external authorities, we may be fortunate to meet kindred spirits or mentors along the way. But even if we don't, the journey remains valid, and its treasures remain accessible.

This leads us to the deeper question: Is it necessary to find a physical teacher, or do teachers appear in the form of synchronicities, challenges, insights, and moments of stillness? Perhaps the higher self—our inner teacher—has always been gently guiding us, leaving breadcrumbs of truth for us to discover when we are truly ready.

I believe all of these are possible. The real turning point is our readiness: the willingness to surrender outdated structures and identities in service of a greater truth. When we are truly ready, the teacher—whether embodied or ethereal—reveals itself not as a goal in itself, but as a mirror reflecting the awakening within us.

"When the student is ready, the teacher will appear" is not just a proverb; it's a spiritual principle. It reminds us that the universe responds to the sincerity of our quest. The "teacher" may come as a mentor, a book, a video, a hardship, or a revelation—each designed to awaken something dormant within. The readiness lies not in seeking externally, but in cultivating the mental, emotional, and spiritual openness to receive.

When we align ourselves with this readiness—when our minds are clear and our hearts are open—we create coherence that magnetizes the right teacher at the right time. In doing so, we evolve. And as we evolve, we influence the collective consciousness, becoming both student and teacher in an eternal dance of transformation.

As Rumi so profoundly expressed, *"What you seek is seeking you."*

Indeed, *when the student is ready, the teacher will appear*—because the readiness itself is the teacher's call.

Chapter 12

Your Identity is Your Reality

By the mirror of your mind, you see,
The world becomes what you believe.
A thought, a name, a silent creed—
Each shapes the life you choose to lead.

If you claim fear, the shadows stay,
But call forth light, and night turns day.
You are not just flesh and bone—
You're soul, you're spark, you're truth unknown.

So wear your truth with clarity,
For your identity births reality.

We live in a world that tells us who we are before we ever have the chance to ask. we are taught how to see ourselves—not through our own understanding, but through the expectations, judgments, and projections of others. Society begins to shape us, assigning roles, attaching labels and setting standards for who we should be. We are defined by our accomplishments and diminished by our failures. We are praised for our strengths and punished for our flaws. Over time, we begin to believe that our identity is something given to us—not something we innately possess.

We experience life through the limited lens of the third-dimensional world, where duality reigns—light and dark, success and failure, love and fear, birth and death. Time is experienced in a straight line, and space becomes the boundary within which our lives unfold. This construct, while essential for navigating the physical world, often becomes a cage. It restricts our sense of self, convincing us that we are subject to forces greater than ourselves—divine powers outside of us, scripting our fate, controlling our destiny. In this paradigm, we begin to live in reaction rather than creation.

We become puppets to the puppeteer, mere creations at the mercy of a creator's whims. We identify with fear that becomes our compass and cling to anything that offers pleasure or momentary relief from the looming awareness that all of it could end at any moment. We get stuck in memories and regrets of the past, dreams and worries of the future—robbing us of the joy found only in the present. We forget our own sovereignty and become characters in someone else's play.

The mask we wear is shaped by desire, achievement, insecurity, failure, and expectation—sculpting the ego-self that helps us navigate this realm, but not the essence of who we truly are. It is a reflection of the fabricated "identity" that is nothing more than a carefully constructed illusion, a story we've repeated so often we begin to believe it's real.

Quantum physics explores reality at its most fundamental level and provides a profound mirror to the metaphysical. It reveals that at the subatomic level, particles exist in states of possibility until they are observed. Reality is not fixed—it is fluid, influenced by attention and awareness. This scientific truth echoes a spiritual one: we are not passive observers of life; we are active participants in its creation. Each thought, each perception, each intention shapes the world we experience.

The very act of looking alters what is seen. It suggests that observation itself influences a quantum system's state. Reality, then, is not fixed, but in some sense created by the very act of observing it. Every quantum measurement gives rise to multiple parallel universes, each reflecting a different possible outcome.

The reality we create in our lives is shaped by what and how we observe. And what grants us the power of observation is the lens through which we choose to see. It is the internal lens we carry—formed by our beliefs, our emotions, our sense of self. If our lens is shaped by fear, we will see a world of limitation. If it is polished by love, we will see infinite possibility. The universe reflects us back to ourselves.

There comes a sacred moment in every soul's journey—a moment when the external noise quiets, the old masks begin to crack, and we are invited to look into the mirror of our being. Not to see the image that others have projected onto us, but to remember the divine truth that has always lived.

The soul was never meant to fit into boxes—it was born to break them. It is not here to conform—it is here to awaken. Our identity is not something we earn, nor something we perform. It is the divine spark within us, waiting to be remembered. It is the essence that has never been broken, never been lost—only forgotten.

When we identify with fear, we build walls, we shrink, we hide. We create a life of survival. But when we choose to identify with love—with the truth of who we are—we become co-creators with the universe. We shape a reality where peace, joy, and abundance are not rare miracles but natural states of being. The question is not, *"What is real?"* but rather, *"What are we aligning with?"* For the essence of our being radiates outward, becoming the very lens through which we experience life.

We are not our past. We are not our pain. We are not even the narrative we've clung to—the one we've rehearsed, revised, and replayed in our minds. We are the awareness the observer—that has witnessed it all. Unchanging. Eternal. Divine.

To truly know ourselves is not to gather more knowledge or layer on more identities—it is to strip away and remove the false, until what remains is pure and sacred truth.

Look within and ask:
Who am I when no one is watching?
Who am I when the applause fades, when the titles fall away, when the striving ceases?
Who am I beyond the fear of being misunderstood, beyond the need to prove or perform?

In that stillness, the answer rises.
I am the breath of God.
I am light wrapped in skin.
I am the echo of eternity, pulsing in the rhythm of a heartbeat.

And when we walk in that knowing—when we embody that truth—the external world begins to shift. The illusions fall away. Mountains move. Peace finds us. Love flows freely. Reality no longer distorts our essence—it begins to mirror our magnificence.

We are not becoming—we are remembering.
And in that remembrance, our identity becomes our reality.

Chapter 13

Healing the Wounded Warrior

I bore the weight of battles past,
With scars that time could never cast.
Each wound a tale, each pain a song,
A path I walked alone so long.

But in the ache, a spark was born,
A softer strength from being torn.
I learned to heal through hands once shaken,
To give the peace I had forsaken.

Now where I fell, I help others rise,
A mirror held to tear-filled eyes.
For even broken hearts can feel—
The power in the will to heal.

A "wounded warrior" is someone who has experienced emotional, psychological, or spiritual wounds that hinder their ability to fully live out their potential and purpose. These wounds may stem from personal struggles, traumatic experiences, or deep internal battles that leave lasting imprints on the soul.

Life in a dualistic reality is often a battleground—especially when we remain unaware of our innate power. The challenges we face can leave us depleted, burdened by invisible wounds that show up as emotional pain, mental exhaustion, or a sense of being broken. Left unhealed, these wounds can ripple outward: passed down through generations as *ancestral trauma*, or absorbed collectively as *shared societal pain*. Ancestral trauma carries the weight of historical suffering, shaping our behaviors and beliefs in unconscious ways. Meanwhile, collective trauma—born from injustices, wars, or cultural suppression—creates a sense of grief, disconnection, and loss of identity that touches entire communities.

In truth, we are all wounded warriors in some form. Struggle is embedded in the density of this human experience. These wounds not only affect our mental and emotional states but also obscure our spiritual connection—blocking our ability to commune with God, feel joy, or live authentically. Christianity offers a powerful archetype in Jesus, the ultimate wounded warrior, whose suffering exemplifies the redemptive power of love and sacrifice. His crucifixion, and the wounds he bore, symbolize the transformative potential of embracing pain with grace. Through Christ Consciousness, we are invited to transmute our own suffering into healing—not only for ourselves, but for the greater whole.

Our journey through this life is part of a sacred initiation—the hero's path within the 3D realm. Struggle, transformation, and transcendence are part of the curriculum. Each time we confront our wounds, learn from them, and rise again, we add to the unified field of consciousness—a sacred reservoir of wisdom available to those in alignment with truth. Healing begins with awareness. It deepens with forgiveness. And it culminates in a spiritual rebirth, where joy, purpose, and wholeness can finally take root.

Spiritual healing is not a linear process; it is a holistic unfolding. It calls us to integrate mind, body, and spirit through practices such as meditation, prayer, energy work, and conscious supplication. True healing addresses not just symptoms, but the root causes—often buried deep within the psyche or inherited from lineage. Through ancestral and collective healing, we gain the power to release inherited burdens and create new, life-affirming narratives for ourselves and our communities.

The essence of a true warrior lies in two qualities: humility and courage. Real courage is the ability to remain open-hearted amidst adversity, to rise after every fall, and to walk with perseverance even when the path is uncertain. From this journey emerges the *Wounded Healer*—an individual who has transmuted personal pain into wisdom, becoming a beacon of empathy and guidance for others. As Carl Jung articulated, the healer's wounds become the very source of their gift: a bridge between suffering and understanding, isolation and connection, despair and redemption.

In embracing our wounds, we awaken our purpose. In healing ourselves, we heal the world. And in becoming wounded warriors turned healers, we stand not as broken beings—but as sacred vessels through which divine light enters, restores, and uplifts all.

Chapter 14

Ancestral Trauma, Karma, and Spiritual Coma

Wounds unspoken, echo deep,
In silent hearts, the shadows sleep.
From blood and bone, the pain is cast,
A legacy bound to heal at last.

Karma weaves through time and space,
Each action etched, no step erased.
The soul forgets, the debt remains,
Till love redeems ancestral chains.

In spirit's sleep, we drift, confined,
Detached from truth, from self, from mind.
But stir we must, from slumber rise,
And meet the dawn with open eyes.

Ancestral trauma, also known as generational or intergenerational trauma, refers to the psychological and emotional wounds passed down through families due to the unresolved trauma of previous generations. These inherited wounds can stem from events such as war, abuse, slavery, displacement, or systemic oppression. The impact is often multi-generational, affecting not only those who experienced the original trauma but also their descendants. These effects can manifest as mental health challenges, behavioral patterns, emotional dysregulation, and even physical ailments.

Trauma is transmitted through several mechanisms. Children may learn maladaptive coping strategies or internalize limiting beliefs by observing the behavior of their caregivers. On a biological level, studies suggest trauma may influence gene expression, altering stress responses in future generations. Collectively, cultural and historical experiences of oppression or injustice also shape the collective psyche, influencing how entire communities relate to themselves and the world.

Examples of intergenerational trauma include patterns of substance abuse, domestic violence, poverty mindsets, and the psychological scars left by racism or war. These burdens often hinder individuals' ability to form healthy relationships, make sound decisions, or experience emotional balance.

Karma, in spiritual philosophy, is the principle of cause and effect—what we sow through our actions, intentions, and thoughts, we eventually reap. It extends beyond a single lifetime, suggesting that our current circumstances may be shaped by the unresolved actions and energy from past lives. Positive actions generate favorable outcomes, while harmful behavior contributes to karmic debt. Karma reminds us of our interconnectedness and the long-reaching consequences of our choices, emphasizing intention as a critical factor in shaping destiny.

Spiritual coma refers to a state of spiritual stagnation or numbness—a disconnection from one's divine essence or spiritual path. Much like a physical coma, this condition implies an unresponsive, dormant spiritual state. It often results from overwhelming life demands, emotional burnout, trauma, or the inherited weight of ancestral suffering and unresolved karma. Many people remain trapped in cycles of lack, fear, or unworthiness, even as they attempt to apply positive thinking or manifestation techniques. Despite their conscious efforts, they feel blocked, as if unseen forces are holding them back.

Breaking free from this loop requires deeper integration of the subconscious wounds that drive these patterns. Healing begins with awareness—acknowledging and honoring the generational pain and karmic imprints we carry. Safe spaces for dialogue, therapeutic support, and spiritual guidance are essential for releasing inherited burdens. By addressing trauma at its root, developing emotional resilience, and reestablishing a meaningful connection to the divine, we awaken from spiritual dormancy and begin to reclaim our authentic power.

In essence, ancestral trauma, karma, and spiritual coma are deeply interconnected threads in the soul's journey. When left unexamined, they create unseen barriers to healing and wholeness. But when consciously brought into the light, they offer profound opportunities for liberation—not just for ourselves, but for the generations before and after us. True transformation begins when we acknowledge the unseen, take responsibility for our healing, and reawaken to the sacred truth of who we really are.

Chapter 15

Shadow Work: Removing the Ego Mask

Beneath the smile, a hidden face,
A fragile mask in time and space.
Worn for praise, to hide the ache,
To guard the soul from hearts that break.

But shadows stir when truth is near,
Exposing wounds we've tucked in fear.
Through inner night, we take the task—
To meet ourselves beyond the mask.

In silent depths, the ego fades,
Revealing light that never shades.
And in that truth, both raw and vast,
We find the self that's free at last.

The ego mask is the social persona we adopt to present ourselves to the world—often a carefully curated identity shaped by external pressures, expectations, and the desire for approval. While it can help us navigate social settings, this mask rarely reflects our true inner self. Instead, it often conceals our authentic nature, hindering self-expression and emotional well-being.

Because the ego is inherently fragile, it relies on this mask to protect its perceived vulnerabilities and maintain a polished image. It craves validation and control, projecting confidence or dominance to influence how others perceive us. In reality, the mask is a defense mechanism—constructed not from strength, but from fear: the fear of exposure, judgment, and inadequacy.

This identification with the ego mask disconnects us from our divine essence, replacing authenticity with illusion. The deeper we attach to roles and appearances, the more we live under the influence of fear—seeking control in a world we feel powerless to navigate. Societal norms reinforce this false self, urging conformity over self-inquiry, masking our truth to maintain superficial harmony.

To dismantle this illusion and return to authenticity, we must confront the very parts of ourselves we've hidden. This is where **shadow work** begins.

Shadow work is the practice of exploring and integrating the unconscious aspects of the self—those repressed emotions, beliefs, and impulses we've deemed unacceptable or unlovable. It invites us to examine the

darker corners of our psyche, to understand how unresolved wounds and conditioned responses shape our thoughts, choices, and relationships.
By courageously facing our shadows, we develop deeper self-awareness and begin to transform unconscious patterns into conscious empowerment. Through tools like journaling, meditation, and introspection, we reveal limiting beliefs and emotional blocks, allowing space for healing, authenticity, and growth.

Shadow work is not just psychological—it is spiritual. It aligns us with our true self by reintegrating all aspects of who we are, not just the parts we prefer to show. As we reclaim these disowned pieces, we move closer to wholeness, experience greater emotional freedom, and cultivate genuine connections with others.

Removing the ego mask through shadow work is a sacred act of liberation. It allows us to step out of illusion and into authenticity, shedding fear and reclaiming our divine power. In doing so, we awaken to the truth that our worth has never depended on how we are perceived, but on how deeply we know and embody who we truly are.

Chapter 16

Over-Analysis Leads to Paralysis

A thought begins, then splits in two,
Each branch demands a closer view.
What if, what then, what might unfold?
The fire of action grows ice-cold.

A thousand paths, none feel quite right,
The mind debates all day and night.
But while the logic twists and spins,
The chance to leap grows paper-thin.

So hush the noise, and take one stride—
For truth reveals when fears subside.

Over analysis paralysis is the inability to make a decision due to excessive overthinking. It's a state of being overwhelmed by the need to make a "perfect" choice, which leads to procrastination, anxiety, and inaction. When trapped in this mindset, we ruminate endlessly, fear making the wrong move, and delay progress. This not only robs us of spontaneity and joy, but it also causes us to miss opportunities aligned with our growth.

Similarly, when we experience *spiritual paralysis*, we become stuck in our soul's journey. Fear, doubt, and a lack of alignment with Divine will prevent us from moving forward. This paralysis is more than just indecision—it is a deep disconnection from our spiritual power. The energies of the soul, mind, heart, will, and body become bound by the illusion that we are powerless, lacking the courage to act on our deepest longings.

This spiritual stagnation often stems from identifying with a limited version of ourselves. When we forget the divine essence within us, we unconsciously give our power away to false idols—whether they be people, beliefs, or material illusions. In seeking answers outside of ourselves, our minds spiral into overanalysis, trying to make sense of chaos without tapping into our inner knowing. This leads us into a victimhood mentality, believing life is happening *to* us rather than *through* us. We become passive actors in a story written by fear, rather than conscious creators of our own divine narrative.

Breaking free from spiritual paralysis requires a return to our true nature. Practices such as meditation, mindfulness, and introspective study can guide us back to self-awareness. These tools allow us to quiet the mind, heal limiting beliefs, and access higher consciousness. As we realign with the Divine and honor the interconnectedness of all life, we begin to see the universe not as something to be feared or analyzed, but as something to be trusted and co-created with.

Through this reconnection, we experience a renewed sense of purpose and direction. Realignment with Divine will brings clarity, peace, and fulfillment. We no longer chase meaning—we embody it. Surrendering personal agendas in favor of divine guidance opens us to deeper insight, a broader awareness of who we truly are, and a sense of participation in a greater unfolding plan.

In this expanded state of consciousness, we come to a profound realization: *we were never separate from the Divine.* As Rumi beautifully said, *"What you seek is already within you."* With heart and mind in coherence, stillness arises. Doubt dissolves. Confusion fades. We no longer merely think—we *know.*

And in this knowing, paralysis ends—because purpose begins.

Chapter 17

What We Resist, Persists

We turn away, deny, defend,
Yet shadows linger to the end.
The more we fight, the more they stay—
Unseen truths won't drift away.

Embrace the dark, the pain, the fear,
And watch them fade when we draw near.
For only when we let things be,
Can we at last be truly free.

As divine beings experiencing a limited human existence, our lives are meant to reflect the fluidity of our true essence—unbounded and luminous—even within the illusion of form and restriction. We are here to shine the light generated from within, illuminating the darkness of this 3D construct and serving as beacons in our collective awakening.

When our souls chose to incarnate in this realm, we agreed to temporarily forget who we truly are. This divine amnesia adds intensity to the game of life and deepens the purpose of expanding consciousness. In doing so, we became fully identified with the ego—the limited self whose primary concern is survival: to dominate or be dominated. This identification led us to succumb to fear, giving rise to illusions of lack, limitation, and separation. Ironically, these illusions become the very fuel that propels our soul's evolution in this lifetime.

Under fear's governance, dissatisfaction and a sense of incompleteness become dominant themes in our lives. To soothe the pain within, we cling to external attachments that offer only fleeting relief. These attachments act as dams, restricting the natural flow of life and blocking our ability to create anew. The result is stagnation—spiritual, emotional, and even physical barrenness.

These limitations—both internal and external—impact not only our growth but also our connection to the Divine. Internally, doubts, fears, and limiting beliefs can paralyze us. For example, a deep-seated fear of failure might prevent someone from stepping into their purpose or embracing spiritual truth. Externally, cultural norms, societal pressures, and religious expectations may push us to conform in ways that feel false or unfulfilling, keeping us disconnected from our authentic path.

At our core, we are consciousness—pure energy. When we incarnate into this physical reality, consciousness too undergoes a form of duality: wave and particle, much like in quantum mechanics. This mirrors how we exist both as unique individuals (particle) and as part of a vast, interconnected whole (wave). The wave aspect symbolizes the boundless field of awareness that connects all beings; the particle aspect reflects our localized, subjective experience.

Quantum mechanics suggests that particles behave as both waves and particles depending on how they are observed. This duality invites compelling parallels with consciousness. The act of observation—awareness itself—collapses potential into form, just as our focused attention shapes our reality. Some theories propose that consciousness plays a direct role in the collapse of the quantum wavefunction, suggesting that reality responds to conscious intent.

This quantum principle also applies to the mechanics of everyday life. In our desperation to escape the suffering of the 3D world, we often resist our current circumstances. But in doing so, we create even more resistance. By opposing what is, we trap it. We reinforce the very conditions we want to change.

The phrase *"what you resist, persists,"* attributed to Carl Jung, encapsulates this truth. When we push against unwanted emotions or realities, we feed them with our energy and attention, causing them to linger or grow stronger. Resistance becomes a form of attachment, tethering us to the very things we wish to be free from.

But here lies the paradox: we are powerful, divine beings with temporary amnesia. Though it may seem like we're trapped in a never-ending loop—reliving the same day, the same story—awakening begins the moment we recognize the pattern. We start to remember. We notice the breadcrumbs of truth scattered along our path, and a deeper realization takes root: there is more to us than we've been led to believe.

As we peel away the layers of illusion, the veil begins to lift. We reclaim our inner power and open the portal to liberation—not by resisting reality, but by flowing with it. We realign with our Divine essence, and this internal transformation reflects outwardly. Resistance dissolves. Attachment loses its grip. Harmony and balance return, unimpeded by fear or control.

Ultimately, we come to see ourselves not as victims of life, but as sovereign beings—victors exercising the authority of our own divinity. Life no longer happens *to* us but *for* us. And in this realization, what we accept transforms.

Chapter 18

We Attract What We Are, Not What We Want

Desires may whisper, hopes may plea,
But mirrors of truth shape destiny.
It's not our wishes the world imparts,
But the echoing pulse of our inner hearts.

The world responds not to our plea,
But to the frequency we choose to be.
Align your soul, let your essence shine—
What you become, you will define.

The Law of Attraction suggests that our thoughts and emotions serve as energetic signals that shape the reality we experience. Rooted in the principle that "like attracts like," it proposes that positive thoughts and emotions draw positive outcomes, while negative ones invite undesirable experiences. According to this philosophy, our internal focus—what we consistently think and feel—directly influences what we attract into our lives.

Our thoughts and emotions emit vibrations that interact with the universe, drawing in experiences that resonate with our energetic state. A positive mindset is thought to manifest more favorable outcomes—such as abundance, well-being, and fulfilling relationships—while negativity tends to perpetuate struggle or dissatisfaction. Advocates often apply this concept to finances, health, relationships, and personal fulfillment, emphasizing the power of clarity, intention, and emotional alignment.

While scientific backing for the Law of Attraction is limited, some parallels are drawn from quantum physics—particularly the idea that everything is energy and that consciousness may influence outcomes. The observer effect in quantum experiments, where an observer alters the result by merely being present, is frequently cited by proponents as a metaphor for how human intention may affect reality. Though intriguing, these interpretations remain speculative and should be approached with discernment.

Importantly, manifestation is not passive. Desires rooted purely in ego, misalignment, or fear often fail to materialize because they are out of sync with one's authentic self and spiritual growth. True attraction comes not merely from what we want, but from who we are at our core. It involves aligning our beliefs, emotions, actions, and environment with our deepest values. A supportive, high-vibrational space—both internally and externally—enhances this process, while a toxic or negative environment may hinder it.

Ultimately, we don't attract what we say we want—we attract what we truly embody. The universe mirrors back our inner truth, not our outer presentation or masked intentions. Our relationships, opportunities, and challenges all serve as reflections of the energy we carry within.

As a team—whether in family, community, or organization—our collective energy becomes a shared field that shapes our joint reality. When we each commit to inner alignment, authenticity, and mutual support, we amplify our power to attract growth, purpose, and transformation not only for ourselves but for the whole. In unity, our vibrational resonance becomes unstoppable.

Chapter 19

Be Still and Know That You Are God

In quiet breath, the truth is near,
Beyond the noise, beyond the fear.
No need to strive, no need to flee—
Just be, and know divinity.

The winds may howl, the waters shake,
Yet in your soul, no storm can break.
Be still, and feel the sacred flame—
You are the Light, the Love, the Name.

Stillness is more than the mere absence of movement; it is a profound state of peace, rest, and tranquility where we reconnect with our deepest self and commune with the higher power that breathes life into all things. In stillness, we are invited to release the relentless grip of external stimuli and inner turmoil, allowing space for a deeper awareness to arise. It is in this sacred pause that transformation becomes possible—where the noise of the world fades and the whisper of the soul grows audible.

Cultivating stillness, particularly in the midst of our hyperactive, fast-paced lives, is both an art and a discipline. It demands intentionality: stepping away from to-do lists, screens, and constant motion to return to the present moment. Stillness asks us to let go—not just physically, but mentally and emotionally as well. It is the practice of releasing our attachments to fleeting thoughts, unruly emotions, and the weight of worldly expectations. In return, we are gifted a serenity that anchors us, a sanctuary within ourselves where clarity and calm reign.

Moreover, stillness serves as a sacred gateway to the spiritual realm. In the quiet, we find a path to the Divine—a deeper connection to the infinite presence that undergirds our existence. Here, in the silence of our being, we may experience guidance, rest, and a profound sense of unity with something greater than ourselves. This connection transcends intellectual place: understanding; it is a lived, felt reality, a knowing that defies words.

Importantly, stillness does not always equate to inactivity. It can be present even amidst movement, as seen in practices like walking meditation, mindful breathing, or the flow state achieved in creative pursuits. True stillness is a mental state—an inner posture of focused presence where we remain attuned to the moment, even as life unfolds around us.

Silence, closely intertwined with stillness, holds its own transformative power. In silence, we rediscover the art of listening: to ourselves, to others, and to the Divine. It sharpens our self-awareness, refines our communication, enhances emotional regulation, and promotes cognitive clarity. Silence becomes fertile ground for profound reflection, fostering deeper relationships and a more resilient spirit.

From this place of stillness and silence, we begin to experience oneness with God—a mystical union with the Source of all being. In many spiritual traditions, this oneness is described as a transcendence of the ego, a merging into the boundless, loving presence that sustains the universe. It is not merely a conceptual belief but a lived experience, a state where division falls away and only unity remains.

The understanding of this oneness varies across religious and philosophical systems. In monotheistic faiths like Christianity and Islam, God is often seen as distinct and separate from humanity—a transcendent Creator. Panentheistic views, however, suggest that while God transcends the universe, God's presence fills all of creation intimately. In pantheistic perspectives, the universe and God are one and the same, with no division between the spiritual and the material. Even scientific principles like quantum entanglement hint at a mysterious interconnectedness underlying all things, echoing ancient spiritual insights into the unity of existence.

Yet, regardless of the doctrine or worldview that resonates with us, the essence remains: to align with the Divine Will is to embrace our true nature. It is to live authentically, embodying the highest expression of who we are meant to be. It calls us beyond the fragmented self to the greater self—a being both fully human and fully divine, whole and complete even in our individuality.

In the end, stillness teaches us that we are not merely isolated fragments adrift in a chaotic world. We are reflections of the Divine, vessels of infinite potential, invited to awaken to the sacred reality within and around us.

Be still, and know—you are God's living expression. In the quiet of your soul, you will find not only peace but the truth of who you have always been.

Chapter 20

Life Happens For You, Not To You

The storms may rage, the skies turn gray,
But each dark cloud guides you on your way.
Not punishment, but paths unfold,
In every trial, a truth is told.

You're not a victim of the tide,
But a soul with strength and light inside.
Life bends and breaks to make you new—
It happens *for* you, to see you through.

The idea that "life happens for you, not to you" invites a transformational shift in mindset—from passive victimhood to empowered participation in our own evolution. Rather than viewing hardships as random misfortunes, this perspective reframes them as necessary catalysts for growth, awakening, and self-discovery.

By adopting this empowering view, we begin to see that every experience—whether joyful or painful—carries a purpose. Life's challenges become not setbacks, but stepping stones. Difficult moments, instead of defining us, refine us. While we may not control every event, we *can* control how we perceive and respond to them. This shift in consciousness not only strengthens resilience but fosters a deeper sense of meaning and direction.

Those who embrace a victim mentality often feel powerless, blaming circumstances or others for their suffering. Trapped in cycles of negativity and helplessness, they wait for life to improve from the outside. This reactive stance stalls progress and reinforces disempowerment. In contrast, a victor mindset acknowledges pain without being ruled by it. It asks, *"What can I learn from this?"* and *"How can I grow through this?"* Victors accept responsibility for their healing and choose to move forward with courage, clarity, and intention.

Faith in a higher power often plays a pivotal role in this transformation. For many, belief in divine guidance offers comfort, strength, and a sense of sacred order amidst chaos. It allows one to trust that every experience, no matter how painful, serves a higher purpose. Those who live with this awareness no longer see themselves as separate from the Divine—but as co-creators of a meaningful journey. They see adversity not as punishment, but as preparation.

Ultimately, the journey from victim to victor is a spiritual path—a movement from fear to faith, from resentment to forgiveness, from helplessness to empowerment. Through this transformation, we come to realize that life is not happening *to* us in cruelty, but *for* us in wisdom. Every experience is a mirror, a message, and a moment of becoming. And in that realization, we awaken to life's greatest gift: the power to choose how we grow.

Life does not simply unfold—it unfolds for you. And when you see it that way, everything changes.

Chapter 21

Dis-ease/Disease:
Symptoms of Spiritual Misalignment

When soul and self no longer align,
The body speaks in silent sign—
A fevered heart, a restless mind,
A cough, a pain, a truth confined.

Not merely flesh that breaks or bends,
But spirit's cry the body sends.
Dis-ease begins where peace once stayed,
A whisper lost, a light delayed.

Realign the breath, recall the whole,
Heal the fracture, feed the soul.
For every ailment seeks release—
In balance waits the path to peace.

Though often used interchangeably, the terms **"dis-ease"** and **"disease"** carry distinct meanings. *Disease* refers to a medically diagnosed condition characterized by specific symptoms and biological dysfunctions. It typically involves a breakdown in the body's physiological systems—triggered by genetics, lifestyle, or environmental factors. In contrast, *dis-ease* is a broader term, pointing to any form of discomfort, whether physical, mental, emotional, or spiritual. It doesn't always involve a diagnosable illness. A sense of restlessness, persistent stress, or a vague emotional unease are all expressions of dis-ease.

While disease is more commonly addressed through clinical medicine, dis-ease opens the door to a more holistic understanding of well-being. Both, however, can stem from underlying disruptions—whether physical imbalances or deeper emotional and spiritual disconnections.

From a spiritual perspective, illness is not just a bodily malfunction but a potential *message* from within. It may reflect misalignments in our emotional life, unresolved trauma, suppressed emotions, or a deeper loss of connection to ourselves, others, or a higher power. Emotions such as anger, grief, or chronic anxiety are increasingly linked with health outcomes, from cardiovascular issues to immune system imbalances. Thus, disease can be the body's final expression of prolonged spiritual misalignment.

The **mind-body-spirit** connection teaches us that these three dimensions are not isolated. Chronic emotional stress can manifest as physical pain; a lack of purpose or spiritual fulfillment may slowly erode vitality. In this light, illness becomes a signal—a spiritual call to examine the deeper layers of our being.

Healing, then, becomes more than just curing symptoms. It becomes a journey inward. A true remedy for both disease and disease must consider the whole person: physically, emotionally, and spiritually. This includes adopting healthier lifestyles—such as balanced nutrition, movement, and stress management—but also engaging in practices that nurture the soul. Meditation, prayer, gratitude, self-reflection, and energy therapies like Reiki or sound healing can restore internal balance and promote lasting wellness.

One emerging paradigm is **quantum healing**, which draws from the notion that all life is energy. This perspective emphasizes how our consciousness—through intention, belief, and vibration—interacts with and shapes our physical reality. Though often debated in the scientific realm, its central idea resonates with ancient wisdom: that we are energetic beings in constant interaction with a greater energetic field.

Ultimately, the goal is **spiritual homeostasis**—a state of alignment between our inner truth and external experience. When our thoughts, emotions, and energy align with our deeper Knowing, we move through life with clarity, peace, and resilience. We stop resisting the present moment and start flowing with it, trusting that healing arises from wholeness, not merely the absence of symptoms.

In the end, both dis-ease and disease serve as mirrors, reflecting our soul's misalignments. They invite us not just to treat, but to listen—to turn inward and realign with our essence. Healing begins when we recognize that every symptom is a message, and every imbalance an opportunity for reconnection. When we answer that call, we step onto the path of true well-being—where dis-ease and disease no longer define us, but awaken us to our deeper truth.

"Dis-ease/Disease: Symptoms of Spiritual Misalignment" reminds us that healing is not just about curing the body, but realigning the spirit.

Chapter 22

Relationships: Our Spiritual Contracts

By soul's design, not chance nor fate,
We meet, we clash, we resonate.
Each heart we touch, each hand we hold,
Fulfills a vow our spirits told.

Through joy or grief, through loss or gain,
We grow through love, we learn through pain.
A mirror, guide, or sacred test—
Each bond a path to manifest.

So bless the ones who cross your way,
For they are souls who chose to stay—
To teach, to heal, to help you see,
The truth of who you're meant to be.

The soul is an unchanging, everlasting essence that transcends physical form—a divine spark that persists beyond the cycle of life and death. Rooted in spiritual traditions like Jainism, Tibetan Buddhism, and Vaishnavism, this understanding of the soul reflects its eternal nature and its continuous relationship with the Divine. These traditions often describe the soul as undergoing a series of incarnations, where each lifetime offers lessons, growth, and opportunities for eventual liberation or enlightenment.

Within this expansive journey, souls are not alone. They travel in constellations known as *soul families*—groups of kindred spirits who share a deep resonance and purpose. Soul family members are bound not by blood, but by energetic and spiritual affinity. They often appear in our lives to offer support, companionship, and profound lessons, guiding us with a sense of familiarity and deep knowing. Encounters with them often feel destined, as though meeting someone we've known across lifetimes.

One form of this spiritual bond is the *karmic contract*—an agreement made between souls prior to incarnation to resolve past-life imbalances, heal wounds, or complete unfinished lessons. These relationships often carry emotional intensity and urgency, catalyzing transformation through both joy and challenge. While karmic contracts can be demanding, they are designed for growth, not punishment. They are sacred opportunities for evolution.

Before each incarnation, it is believed that souls collaborate in the higher realms to outline the key elements of their upcoming lives. These *pre-birth agreements* include specific relationships, experiences, and challenges necessary for spiritual advancement. In this blueprint, certain souls may take on the roles of soulmates or twin flames—mirrors and companions chosen to awaken, challenge, and elevate us. While these contracts are divinely inspired, they coexist with the principle of free will. We retain the power to choose how we respond to the lessons embedded in each connection.

Soul contracts come in many forms—divine twin flames, karmic partners, and romantic soulmates among them. But whether comforting or difficult, each relationship invites us into deeper understanding of ourselves and our purpose. They are vehicles for teaching us unconditional love, surrender, forgiveness, strength, and compassion. When embraced consciously, they become pathways for transcending limitation and embodying our highest truths.

In this human experience, relationships often appear to be shaped by chance or circumstance. We celebrate the blissful ones as gifts and lament the painful ones as misfortune. We rarely consider that both types may be fulfilling spiritual agreements carefully designed to serve our growth. As these relationships unfold, they become mirrors—reflecting back to us our beliefs, fears, patterns, and capacity for love. In doing so, they shape our identity and influence how we navigate the physical world.

However, a moment inevitably arises in our journey when we begin to awaken—when the soul whispers through intuition, dreams, or synchronicities, reminding us of our eternal nature. As we remember who we truly are—immortal beings having a finite experience—we begin to see relationships not as burdens or coincidences, but as sacred contracts crafted for our evolution. We realize that every interaction is part of a grand cosmic choreography, and every soul we meet is a reflection of the divine within us.

When we awaken to the spiritual essence of our relationships, we transcend the illusion of separation and reclaim the wisdom of our soul's journey. We understand that every bond—no matter how brief or intense—is purposeful. Our encounters are not random, but resonant; not chaotic, but choreographed. Relationships become portals through which we recognize the Divine in ourselves and in others. In honoring our spiritual contracts, we release judgment, reclaim harmony, and walk the path of conscious evolution—together, as one interconnected soul family, dancing in divine rhythm across time and space.

Chapter 23

Kindred Spirits: Our Soulful Connections

In silence they enter, no need for a name,
A spark in the soul, a familiar flame.
No past to recall, yet known from the start,
They speak to the depths of a wide-open heart.

No mask is needed, no words to defend,
Just presence that heals, a soul's dearest friend.
Together they walk, though paths may divide,
Their essence remains, like the ocean and tide.

For time cannot bind what spirit aligns—
Kindred souls meeting across sacred lines.
A whisper from lifetimes, a nod from above,
Reminding us all—we are held in love.

The journey of awakening is often deeply personal—and at times, profoundly lonely. As individuals go through spiritual and personal evolution, they may feel isolated or disconnected from the world around them. This sense of solitude often arises from a shift in values, beliefs, and worldviews that no longer align with the people or environments they once felt at home in.

As we grow in self-awareness, we naturally begin to shed old identities and patterns that no longer serve us. This process, while liberating, can be misunderstood by others who have not undergone similar transformations. Relationships that were once fulfilling may begin to feel out of sync. Activities that once brought joy may lose their meaning. In the solitude of this metamorphosis, many are called inward, entering a phase of deep introspection and spiritual seeking.

Navigating this solitary path requires grace and resilience. Embracing mindfulness helps ground us during the instability that often accompanies inner change. Cultivating presence allows us to find peace amid uncertainty. While the process may feel isolating, it is not meant to be permanent. Along the way, we often encounter *kindred spirits*—souls who recognize us not just for who we are, but for who we are becoming.

Kindred spirits are not bound by bloodlines or shared histories. They can appear at any stage of life—briefly or for the long haul—and their presence can be transformative. They offer a sense of being seen, understood, and accepted. These connections transcend surface-level interactions and instead operate on a soul level. Some believe these spirits are part of our soul tribe—beings with whom we've shared lifetimes and sacred contracts long before incarnating. Others feel that kindred spirits may be parallel versions of ourselves, intersecting from different timelines, explaining the uncanny sense of familiarity they often bring.

The presence of a kindred spirit can be healing. With them, we feel safe to express our emotions, share our dreams, and explore our fears without fear of judgment. They reflect back to us our highest potential and gently guide us toward our growth. Their intuitive understanding and shared values serve as a compass when navigating life's crossroads. These bonds are often effortless, unburdened by complexity, and anchored in authenticity.

Such soulful connections are not necessarily romantic—they are deeper, subtler, and often more enduring. They resonate on the same vibrational frequency, fostering harmony, mutual growth, and a sense of belonging. The energy exchange is reciprocal and nourishing, offering support through life's inevitable challenges.

In a world where surface connections abound, kindred spirits remind us that true connection is soul-deep. They are the quiet affirmations from the universe that we are not alone on our path. Whether they stay for a season or a lifetime, their presence leaves an indelible mark on our journey.

Kindred spirits are not just companions—they are reflections of the love, truth, and divinity within us. They appear when we are ready to remember who we truly are. In their presence, we find resonance, recognition, and reassurance. And in that sacred space between souls, we are reminded that while the path to awakening may begin in solitude, it ultimately leads us back into the arms of soulful connection—where we are seen, known, and loved beyond words.

Chapter 24

Spirit Guides: Our Divine Helpers

Whispers in silence, gentle and true,
Guiding our steps in all that we do.
Unseen hands through trials they steer,
Speaking in dreams, felt when we're near.

Feathers and signs, a shimmer of light,
They walk beside us through shadow and night.
Not bound by time, nor flesh, nor fear—
Our soul's companions, always near.

Spirit guides are non-physical beings believed to offer guidance and support throughout the human experience. Often described as souls or light beings who have attained a higher state of consciousness, they assist individuals in navigating life's challenges and realizing their full potential.

These guides can manifest in a variety of forms—ancestral spirits, animal totems, inner voices, visions, or a quiet but persistent sense of knowing. Some are recognized as angels, Archangels, Ascended Masters, or even nature spirits. What they share in common is a higher vibrational frequency, enabling them to communicate subtly—through intuition, dreams, synchronicities, or symbolic physical events.

Many spiritual traditions suggest that each of us is assigned a team of spirit guides at birth—helpers who walk with us, unseen, throughout our lives. Others believe these guides appear only when needed, stepping forward during moments of transition, hardship, or spiritual growth.

Communication with spirit guides often requires a quieted mind, discernment, and trust. Their messages may come in response to unspoken questions or as protective warnings. Whether it's a flickering lamp, a book falling at just the right moment, or the sudden appearance of a stranger bearing needed insight—these signs remind us that we are never truly alone. Even in our darkest hours, we are listened to.

The idea of spirit guides is deeply linked with the concept of *oneness*, a foundational truth in many spiritual teachings. Oneness suggests that all beings are interconnected, flowing from the same source of divine consciousness. Spirit guides, then, are not external saviors, but extensions of this shared soul essence—

helpers from the spirit realm cheering us on through the highs and lows of our hero's journey.

Some guides may belong to our soul group—souls who have shared lifetimes with us in various forms. Though they may not currently be embodied, they walk beside us, aligned in purpose and quietly influencing our path. In some cases, we may even have served as spirit guides for others in previous lifetimes. In the vast expanse of eternity, all roles are fluid, and all beings are deeply connected.

The human experience is a brave descent into form and limitation. It requires forgetting who we truly are, only to slowly awaken to that truth once more. This process of remembering—of returning to the essence of our divine nature—is the very purpose of the soul's journey. Spirit guides serve as gentle reminders of that truth, offering subtle nudges to help us rise above fear, illusion, and forgetfulness.

Like an eaglet raised among chickens, we may forget our wings and our sky-bound heritage. But our spirit guides, ever faithful, remind us that we were born to soar.

In the end, spirit guides are not just helpers—they are divine allies who reflect the deeper truth of who

we are: infinite, interconnected, and guided by love. They are, indeed, our divine helpers.

Chapter 25

Breathwork: Our Connection to the Divine

Inhale the stars, exhale the night,
Within each breath, a spark of light.
A sacred rhythm, soft and true,
The soul remembers what it knew.

Through rise and fall, the silence speaks,
In stillness found, the wisdom peaks.
Each breath a bridge, each pause a prayer,
Divine is found in inner air.

Breathwork is the intentional practice of altering breathing patterns to influence mental, physical, and emotional states. As a form of mindfulness, it involves conscious control of the breath to promote relaxation, reduce stress, or enhance focus. Techniques such as deep, rhythmic, or focused breathing are employed to achieve these outcomes.

The pattern and depth of our breath have a direct physiological impact on oxygenation, heart rate, ventilation, and blood pressure. For instance, breathing slowly—at about six breaths per minute—can reduce the chemoreceptor reflex response to hypercapnia (high CO_2) and hypoxia (low oxygen), compared to normal spontaneous breathing at around fifteen breaths per minute. This slower rhythm activates the amygdala, the brain's center for emotional regulation, helping to diminish negative emotions while fostering positive mood and cognitive clarity.

When we experience stress or anxiety, our bodies instinctively enter a state of fight or flight, driven by the sympathetic nervous system. Breathwork counteracts this by stimulating the parasympathetic nervous system, which signals the brain that we are safe. In turn, the brain communicates this safety to the body, allowing it to relax and return to a state of balance.

Mindfulness, a psychological practice of paying non-judgmental attention to the present moment, aligns closely with breathwork. It encourages observing thoughts, feelings, and bodily sensations without getting entangled in them. Through mindfulness, we focus on our immediate sensory experience, let go of judgments, and respond to emotions with curiosity and compassion rather than reactivity.

Breathwork becomes especially profound when approached as a holistic practice, integrating body, mind, and spirit. Like meditation or prayer, it can deepen our awareness and enhance our connection to something greater than ourselves. The breath serves as an anchor, drawing us into the present and opening a doorway to the sacred. Through mindful breathing, we cultivate clarity, calmness, and a spiritual sense of being part of a vast, interconnected universe.

Advanced breathwork modalities, such as Holotropic Breathwork and Conscious Connected Breathing, can even induce altered states of consciousness. By engaging specific breathing patterns, these techniques regulate the nervous system and expand awareness, facilitating emotional release, self-discovery, and potentially transpersonal experiences that feel deeply spiritual or divine in nature.

In essence, breathwork is more than a tool for well-being—it is a sacred bridge that links body and spirit, grounding us in the present while opening us to the Divine. Through each conscious breath, we remember that divinity resides not only beyond us, but within us.

Chapter 26

Synchronicity: The Cosmic Nudge

A thought, a sign, a whispered breeze,
A moment's glance that aims to tease—
Not chance, but threads of time aligned,
A map the cosmos leaves behind.

You think, it comes. You feel, it shows.
A ripple deep where silence flows.
The outer mirrors what's within,
A sacred dance where truths begin.

So pause and see the stars converge,
In every nudge, a soul's new surge.
Not fate, not luck, but light in play—
The Universe guiding your way.

Synchronicity refers to seemingly meaningful coincidences—events that occur simultaneously and feel connected, despite lacking an obvious causal relationship. These are not mere accidents of time and place, but moments imbued with personal or collective significance. The link between such events is not about cause and effect; rather, it's about *meaning*.

The concept of synchronicity was introduced by psychologist Carl Jung, who saw it as a reflection of a unifying consciousness operating through the collective unconscious. He proposed that these meaningful coincidences serve as a form of communication between the psyche and the greater whole, offering insights into the deeper workings of the mind and the universe. From a psychological standpoint, synchronicity becomes a bridge between the conscious self and the unseen forces that shape reality.

However, many scientists explain these experiences through cognitive biases and statistical likelihoods. Confirmation bias—the tendency to notice events that confirm existing beliefs—can make unrelated events appear connected. Similarly, people often underestimate the probability of coincidental events, leading them to ascribe meaning where there may be none. This is closely related to *spurious correlation*, where events appear linked due to coincidence, without any causal connection.

Despite these skeptical views, synchronicity continues to be a profound experience for many. Common examples include thinking of someone just before they call, seeing repeated numbers or symbols, hearing song lyrics that feel deeply personal, encountering meaningful moments in nature, or having dreams that seem to foreshadow future events.

Interestingly, some interpretations draw from quantum physics, which explores the strange behaviors of particles at subatomic levels. Concepts like entanglement and nonlocality hint at connections that transcend time and space. Some theorists suggest that these phenomena could offer a physical analogy—or even a basis—for synchronicity, proposing that consciousness itself might influence the quantum field.

In the context of spiritual awakening, synchronicities are often seen as signs of alignment with a greater universal intelligence. They act as gentle nudges from the cosmos, affirming that one's inner state is harmonizing with external circumstances. Such moments can inspire reflection, clarity, and a deeper understanding of one's path.

As we become more attuned to synchronicities, we learn to recognize their subtle guidance. Far from being random, they may represent affirmations of our inner truths, symbols of transformation, or calls to action. Through mindfulness and inner awareness, we sharpen our ability to perceive these signs, using them as tools for personal growth, spiritual evolution, and deeper connection with the universe.

Ultimately, synchronicity invites us to live in dialogue with the cosmos—to notice the whispers between the lines of ordinary life and to trust the invisible threads weaving through our experiences. Whether seen as divine guidance, quantum mystery, or symbolic reflection, these cosmic nudges remind us that life is not just a sequence of events, but a meaningful dance between the seen and the unseen. By staying open, curious, and aware, we align ourselves with a greater rhythm, allowing synchronicity to become a sacred compass on the journey of the soul.

Chapter 27

Imagination: The Magic Wand of Creation

By thought it stirs, unseen, yet bold,
A silent spark, a dream retold.
It paints the skies with colors rare,
And builds new worlds from whispered air.

It bends the stars, rewrites the sea,
Unlocks the truth of what could be.
A wand unseen, yet full of might—
It turns the dark to dancing light.

So hold it high, this gift divine,
And shape your world by soul's design

Imagination is the mind's ability to create ideas, images, and scenarios that transcend present reality. It allows us to envision what has never been seen, to dream beyond what is, and to shape possibilities before they manifest in the physical world. Whether drawing from memory or constructing entirely new visions, imagination empowers us to bridge the gap between thought and experience.

From a neuroscience perspective, imagination is not a passive daydream but an active mental process involving a sophisticated interplay of brain regions. Key areas include the **dorsolateral prefrontal cortex**, responsible for planning and decision-making; the **hippocampus**, which aids both memory recall and future envisioning; and the **parietal cortex**, which supports spatial reasoning and mental imagery. Together, these systems form a neural network that enables us to simulate, explore, and even rehearse reality—before it unfolds.

The age-old phrase, *"Imagination is magic,"* captures the transformative essence of this inner faculty. Like a wand in the hands of a wizard, imagination has the power to influence not only our inner world but also the world around us. It fuels creativity, innovation, and visionary thinking. It helps us solve problems, overcome limitations, and bring into being that which has only lived in the mind.

In fact, the imagination doesn't just entertain fantasies—it influences behavior, emotion, and outcome. When we vividly imagine a scenario, our brains can react as if it were real, affecting our physiology and emotional state. Athletes use this to mentally rehearse victory. Artists employ it to birth masterpieces. Leaders use it to envision change. In each case, imagination becomes the seed from which reality grows.

This power also echoes in the realm of **quantum physics,** a domain where much of what exists is invisible to the senses. The abstract nature of subatomic phenomena often defies logic and direct perception. Yet through imagination, scientists construct mental models of particles, waves, and energy fields that allow them to explore the unseen dimensions of existence. Imagination thus becomes a bridge between the known and the unknown, the measurable and the mysterious.

Nowhere is this more evident than in the **Law of Attraction**, a principle rooted in the idea that like attracts like on an energetic level. Imagination is the engine of this law—it enables us to visualize our goals, embody our desires, and radiate the frequency of our intentions. By consistently imagining ourselves in states of joy, abundance, or success, we harmonize our thoughts and emotions with our aspirations. This alignment, in turn, draws corresponding opportunities, people, and circumstances into our lives.

Ultimately, imagination is boundless. It knows no restrictions of time, space, or material constraint. This infinite potential makes it one of the most powerful tools we possess. It allows us to see what could be—not just what is—and in doing so, positions us not merely as passive observers of reality, but as **active creators** of it.

In a world often governed by logic and empirical evidence, imagination reminds us of our intrinsic power to envision, transform, and create. It is not a frivolous escape from reality, but the very blueprint of it. Through imagination, we gain the ability to reframe the past, reshape the present, and reimagine the future. It is the silent architect of every invention, every movement, every miracle.

To wield imagination is to hold the magic wand of creation, a tool available to all, limited by none. When we dare to imagine boldly and believe deeply, we unlock the divine creative force within us. In that moment, we don't just imagine reality—we begin to *create* it.

Chapter 28

Dreams: Whispers from the Subconscious

In silent sleep, the soul takes flight,
Through shadowed depths and realms of light.
Each dream a whisper, soft and true,
A secret path the spirit knew.

Dreams are images, thoughts, and sensations that unfold in the mind during sleep, often in the REM (Rapid Eye Movement) stage. They can be vivid or vague, realistic or surreal, comforting or disturbing. While the precise purpose of dreaming remains a mystery, both scientific and psychological theories suggest that dreams play a significant role in memory processing, emotional regulation, and cognitive development.

From a neurological perspective, dreams may support memory consolidation, transferring experiences from short-term to long-term storage. Brain activity during learning is often replayed during sleep, and this replay may surface in dream content. Additionally, REM sleep is strongly associated with emotional processing. Dreams can provide a safe space for the mind to explore and resolve intense emotions, especially those linked to trauma or significant life events. Through dreaming, we may engage in emotional rehearsal, experiencing difficult scenarios with less psychological distress than in waking life.

Cognitive scientists propose that dreams may also simulate real-life situations and serve as mental "rehearsals" for future events. This theory suggests dreams prepare us for potential threats or help us navigate complex social or emotional challenges. In this way, dreams function as a type of internal simulation that sharpens our problem-solving abilities and creative thinking.

Beyond biology, dreams have long fascinated psychologists and mystics alike for their potential to reveal hidden aspects of the self. Sigmund Freud, for example, viewed dreams as a window into the unconscious—a space where repressed desires, memories, and motivations come to light through symbolic imagery. Carl Jung expanded this view by exploring the archetypal and spiritual dimensions of dreams, suggesting they connect us with a deeper layer of the psyche and the collective unconscious.

Dreams are deeply personal and subjective. Symbols and scenarios that appear may not hold universal meanings but instead reflect the dreamer's individual experiences and emotional landscape. A recurring image of water, for instance, might signify fear to one person and serenity to another, depending on their unique associations.

Recurring dreams, in particular, often point to unresolved inner conflicts or unacknowledged emotions. These persistent narratives may act as messages from the subconscious, urging self-reflection or emotional healing. Lucid dreaming—when one becomes aware of the dream state—can provide a conscious gateway into the subconscious, allowing dreamers to actively engage with their inner world and extract deeper insights.

Despite differing perspectives—ranging from theories of random neural firings to wish fulfillment—most agree that dreams offer a unique vantage point into the mind's inner workings. Whether viewed through the lens of science, psychology, or spirituality, dreams are more than nighttime entertainment—they are a powerful tool for growth, self-awareness, and transformation.

In a world increasingly dominated by logic and reason, dreams remain one of the few untouched realms where the soul speaks freely. To listen to our

dreams is to listen to ourselves—our fears, our hopes, our hidden truths. In their mystery lies the potential for profound understanding and healing.

Chapter 29

Dark Night of the Soul: Bottomless Chasm

Into the depths the spirit falls,
Where silence wraps the shadowed walls.
No light to guide, no path to see,
Just echoes of what used to be.

A hollow ache, a sacred tear,
The soul confronts its deepest fear.
Yet in that void, so vast and wide,
The self is stripped of all its pride.

From ashes cold, a spark ignites,
To birth the truth from endless nights.
For only through the darkest flame,
The soul remembers whence it came.

There comes a point in the soul's journey where a profound purification must take place—a stripping away of all that no longer serves the emerging self. This inner transformation is akin to a diamond being shaped by a master cutter, who alone envisions the brilliance hidden within the rough. Such a process is neither gentle nor quick. It is often marked by trial, isolation, and emotional desolation. Yet, it is a sacred initiation—essential for revealing the authentic self long obscured by societal conditioning and the ego's protective layers, formed out of fear rather than love.

This experience is known as the **Dark Night of the Soul**.

Mystic and poet Saint John of the Cross coined the term to describe a stage of passive purification within spiritual development. In his treatise *Dark Night*, he portrays this phase as following illumination—a time when God's presence has been felt, but not yet fully integrated. The soul, having glimpsed the divine, must now undergo a necessary stripping away of illusions and attachments, paving the path toward union with the Divine.

In contemporary language, the "dark night" has become a metaphor for the deep, painful crises of faith, identity, or purpose that shake the foundations of our being. It is a season of confusion, emptiness, and disconnection. One may feel as though they are plummeting into a bottomless chasm with no end in sight. But this descent is not destruction—it is dismantling. The dismantling of ego, of false identities, of expectations that no longer align with the soul's truth.

This journey of "unselfing" demands surrender—letting go of attachments to who we thought we were, to familiar roles and comforts. It can feel like death, but it is the death of illusion. From this inner void, the true self is born. What emerges is not a return to the old, but a rebirth into greater authenticity, deeper purpose, and a more profound connection to a higher power.

The dark night often arises in the wake of life-altering events: the death of a loved one, the collapse of a relationship, a personal awakening that reveals the hollowness of a former life. Pain, grief, loneliness, and anger are common companions in this passage. Yet, those undergoing this transformation often find that emotions like hatred, jealousy, and guilt begin to lose their grip. Their rising awareness prevents full identification with these lower states.

Spiritual awakening may bring about emotional shifts, heightened sensitivity, and even physical symptoms such as fatigue or headaches. These are signs of a deeper recalibration at work. There is no fixed timeline for this process—it may last weeks, months, or longer. What matters most is surrendering to the rhythm of the soul, trusting that there is purpose in the pain and wisdom in the waiting.

Navigating the dark night calls for radical acceptance, self-compassion, and an openness to guidance from inner wisdom or divine presence. Practices such as meditation, prayer, journaling, or seeking spiritual counsel can provide anchoring in the midst of inner storms.

Eventually, dawn follows the darkness.

Those who emerge from the dark night often report a profound shift in perception. They feel lighter, more aligned, and deeply connected to their true nature. A new sense of meaning arises—one no longer tethered to egoic striving, but rooted in love, service, and inner peace. The world is seen through fresh eyes, as if veils have lifted to reveal the sacredness of each moment.

The **Dark Night of the Soul** is not the end—it is the threshold.

It is the bottomless chasm that breaks us open, not to destroy, but to make space for rebirth. In its depths, we confront our shadows, surrender our illusions, and rediscover our light. This sacred unraveling brings us home to ourselves and to the divine essence within all things.

For it is in the dark night that the soul, once lost, remembers how to shine.

Chapter 30

The Void: The In-Between of Desire and Manifestation

In silence deep, where dreams still sleep,
Desire floats but does not weep.
No form, no name, yet pulses grow—
A seed unseen begins to glow.

Between the wish and world made real,
The void holds space for soul to feel.
Not empty, but a sacred womb,
Where thought prepares to break its tomb.

Trust the dark, the pause, the still—
It shapes the heart, aligns the will.
For in that hush, the truth is spun—
The birth of all that's yet begun.

As incarnate beings in this 3D construct, we all carry desires in one form or another. This is the rule of the game: to surrender and fully immerse ourselves in the illusion of separation from our true divine self — a self that is already whole and lacking in nothing. These desires serve as anchors, guiding us through the vast, multilayered experiences of form until we reach the chapter of remembering and begin retracing the path of awakening to who we truly are.

Desires often arise from deeply embedded, unconscious beliefs rooted in lack, limitation, and separation. These beliefs shape our experiences of polarity, making them intense and impactful — the necessary catalysts for learning, evolving, and maturing. They give structure to our linear journey, where we move through lessons and stages of development. We experience the full spectrum of love and hate, joy and sorrow, success and failure, gain and loss. We identify with the cycles of birth, growth, aging, and the eventual death of the physical body. We feel deeply in our relationships with ourselves and others, undergoing countless inner transformations until we eventually find ourselves turning inward, transcending illusion, and reuniting the Divine with the human self.

Throughout this transformation, we come to realize we have never been alone. Everything has always been part of a co-creative process — a dance between our higher and lower selves and the souls around us, each playing out their own unique and sacred individuality.

Yet, within the illusion, we often feel disempowered, believing that the forces capable of shaping our reality exist outside of us. We unknowingly submit to the control of the reptilian mindset — manifesting from lack and confusion, then questioning why we fail. What we fail to see is that everything we desire already exists within the void, available without limit. The only requirement is that we match the vibrational frequency of what we seek.

So, what is the void?

The void is a space beyond form, identity, or content — a realm untouched by the constructs of mind or matter. It is the sensation of dissonance between our real self and the egoic self we've constructed in its place. It is our authentic self calling out from behind the masks we wear. Spiritually, the void is a sacred emptiness, a liminal space of transition, where familiar identities and beliefs dissolve. It is a meditative state where thoughts drift by without judgment, a lucid threshold where the mind is awake but the body is at rest — a place from which we can access absolute, boundless potential. It is the womb of creation, where from no-thing, all things arise.

Access to the void is natural. It is our birthright. The void lives within us, and we are always drawing from it through the Law of Attraction, whether or not we are aware of it. This law reminds us that our focus determines what we magnetize into our experience. Positive emotions and thoughts align us with positive outcomes, while negativity begets more of the same. The void is beyond duality — it does not distinguish between good or bad, right or wrong. It mirrors our inner state: we attract who we are.

A common misconception is that simply assuming the feeling of the wish fulfilled is enough to manifest it. But without entering the void — that silent, relaxed state free of limiting thought — the process lacks its true power. The void must be entered with intention and belief, for it is within this state that we tap into our innate potential and embody our desires as if they already exist. Techniques such as meditation, breathwork, visualization, and affirmations can help us access this space. But it is our belief in the void and our unwavering intention that allow its magic to unfold.

The void is not always comfortable. It can feel like a stripping away — a necessary part of awakening. We must face the raw truth of who we are by dismantling the ego's false identities. Only then can we open the door to deep introspection and lasting transformation. In this surrender, the integrated self emerges — a blank slate, a fertile womb of potentiality. From this sacred space, all things become possible.

To dwell in the void is to stand on the edge of creation itself — neither grasping nor resisting, but simply becoming. In this quiet space between desire and manifestation, we meet the essence of who we truly are: infinite creators awakening from the dream of separation. The void does not ask us to do more, but to remember — to feel, to align, and to allow. From the stillness of the void, we birth new realities, shaped not by force but by the gentle, sovereign power of presence.

Chapter 31

Gratitude: Gateway to Abundance

Gratitude, a seed so small,
Planted deep within us all.
It grows in hearts, a light to see,
A gateway to abundance, free.

In thankfulness, our hearts align,
Attracting blessings, pure, divine.
With every act, a ripple spreads,
Opening paths where joy is led.

So let us cherish, day by day,
The gift of thanks in every way.
For in this grace, we come to find,
Abundance flows, in heart and mind.

Everyone desires abundance—whether in tangible forms like money, possessions, prestige, or power, or in the intangible treasures of love, respect, friendships, and fulfillment. We often believe that abundance is the fuel propelling us through life, the ultimate goal we must achieve to consider our journey a success. There is nothing inherently wrong with this pursuit—especially as we approach life's later chapters, when physical limitations remind us of the importance of having resources to sustain our well-being and comfort.

Yet, despite this universal yearning, how many of us truly feel abundant? Is abundance reserved only for the upper three percent of society? If so, it is disheartening to think that the remaining ninety-seven percent must live in scarcity. But perhaps the question runs deeper: is abundance something quantifiable at all, and who defines the measure of "enough"? If the bar is set so high that most people fall short, then surely, there is a flaw in the very design of this belief system.

I hold the conviction that we are all meant to live abundantly. Created in the image and likeness of the Divine, we are not just passive recipients of life—we are creators of it. Whether through the lens of mysticism and the law of attraction, or the scientific lens of quantum physics, we find the same empowering truth: reality responds to the observer. If the quantum field collapses into form according to our observation, why not choose to observe abundance?

In theory, it appears to be a simple equation of cause and effect. Yet in practice, many still feel trapped in lack. Perhaps the challenge lies not in abundance itself, but in our perception and relationship to it.

By definition, abundance is a plentiful supply, often suggesting more than enough. It encompasses material wealth, resources, and intangible blessings like love, joy, and inner peace. Spiritual abundance, in particular, is about recognizing the richness of life itself—a state of wholeness that transcends material counts. When we expand our understanding of abundance beyond material accumulation, we open ourselves to the profound truth that abundance already exists, surrounding us in countless forms. The trouble is, we often fail to see it.

If abundance is not a matter of definition, then perhaps it is an issue of recognition. Too often, we overlook the blessings before us because our minds are caught in regret over the past or anxiety about the future. We lose the ability to fully enjoy the present moment, where abundance quietly resides.

It is both our birthright and our responsibility to live abundantly as individualized expressions of the Divine. Yet we frequently operate from a scarcity mindset, striving for abundance out of desperation rather than inspiration. To attract abundance, we must first heal our relationship with it. Scarcity thinking can be deeply rooted in ancestral wounds and collective traumas, which must be acknowledged and integrated. Only then can we expand our capacity to receive the fullness of life.

We live in an energetic universe governed by vibration and frequency. Everything—our thoughts, emotions, even the smallest particle—vibrates. According to the laws of energy, we attract not opposites, but that which matches our own frequency. Simply put: we attract who we are. Our external reality mirrors our inner state of being. And abundance, existing at a high vibrational frequency, requires us to elevate our own energy to meet it. One of the most powerful portals to such elevation is gratitude.

Gratitude is more than an emotion—it is energy in motion. It is the conscious recognition and appreciation of the goodness in our lives. Gratitude embodies three essential qualities: awareness, appreciation, and thankfulness.

But why is gratitude so essential? Because it enhances our well-being, fosters positive emotions, and diminishes stress. A regular practice of gratitude strengthens our relationships, builds resilience, and leads to a deeper sense of fulfillment. Is this not the very essence of an abundant life?

Even Christ's profound teaching echoes this truth: *"Seek ye first the kingdom of God, and all these things shall be added unto you."* The kingdom of God is within us—found in our alignment with the Divine and our realization that we are divine beings having a human experience. This alone is cause for unending gratitude and celebration of life in all its forms.

Gratitude and abundance are not separate forces but intimately connected energies. When we cultivate gratitude, we open ourselves to abundance in its many manifestations. By focusing on what we already have and truly appreciating it, we create a powerful magnetism that attracts more of the same.

How Gratitude Leads to Abundance:

- **Shifting Perspective:** Gratitude turns our focus from scarcity to sufficiency, revealing the abundance that already exists.

- **Attracting Positive Experiences:** Expressing gratitude signals to the universe our readiness to receive more blessings.

- **Rewiring the Brain:** Gratitude trains our minds to seek positivity, cultivating an abundant mindset.
- **Creating a Cycle of Abundance:** Gratitude creates momentum, setting into motion a virtuous cycle of growing abundance in wealth, health, relationships, and joy.

Finally, abundance is not a distant goal to chase, but a present reality to embrace. It begins with a simple yet profound shift in perception: recognizing that we are already immersed in blessings. Gratitude is the gateway through which abundance flows freely. When we choose gratitude as our daily posture, we step into harmony with the abundant universe, and life, in all its fullness, responds in kind.

So let us live in gratitude and watch as the floodgates of abundance open wide.

Chapter 32

Compassion: Hallmark of the Integrated Soul

In silence deep, where ego falls,
The soul awakens, heeds love's calls.
No need for praise, no fear to shield—
Its tender truth is gently revealed.

It sees the wound behind the veil,
It feels the storm beneath the tale.
With open heart and steady grace,
It meets all pain in sacred space.

No judgment sharp, no prideful role—
Compassion flows from the whole soul.
In giving light, it becomes more whole—
The hallmark of the integrated soul.

Compassion is more than a sympathetic feeling—it's a profound emotional response to another's suffering, paired with an earnest desire to alleviate it. Unlike empathy, which allows us to feel *with* someone, compassion moves us to *act* on their behalf. It's empathy in motion, an awakened heart in service of healing. Compassion can be understood in different relational forms:

- **Familial compassion** – the innate care we feel for our loved ones in times of pain.

- **Familiar compassion** – the concern extended to friends, colleagues, and those we have a connection with.

- **Stranger compassion** – the purest form, offered to those we do not know, simply because they too are human and hurting.

In spiritual and philosophical traditions, compassion is often revered as a sacred gift—a divine impulse that transcends the ego and links us to the suffering and joy of others. It's a signpost of a soul awakening to its interconnected nature.

But perhaps the most essential, and often overlooked, form of compassion is **compassion toward oneself**.

Self-compassion means treating yourself with the same tenderness and care you would offer a beloved friend during a time of struggle. It is acknowledging your pain without judgment, extending empathy inward, and holding space for healing rather than criticism. It recognizes suffering not as a personal failure, but as a universal human experience.

There are three foundational elements to self-compassion:

- **Self-kindness** – Being gentle and nurturing with yourself, especially in moments of perceived failure.

- **Common humanity** – Understanding that imperfection is not a flaw but a shared human trait that connects us all.

- **Mindfulness** – Observing our emotions and thoughts without judgment, allowing them to be, without being swept away by them.

The irony, however, is that many of us, myself included, find it easier to offer compassion to others than to ourselves. We become our own harshest critics, trapped in a cycle of self-judgment and doubt. We analyze our choices, question our worth, and dwell on our shortcomings. This inner voice is often not truly ours—

it's a product of societal conditioning, past hurts, and outdated narratives imposed on us from the outside.

We carry the scars of betrayal and rejection, and those wounds shape our internal dialogue. These unresolved traumas, though deeply personal, form part of a collective pattern shared across humanity. We become actors in a script we didn't write, following the direction of unseen forces. But the real question is: *Who is directing the show?*

If left unhealed, trauma embeds itself in our subconscious, dictating how we move through the world. It becomes so familiar that we mistake it for truth, shaping our responses and beliefs within this dense 3D reality.

As individualized expressions of the Divine, we were meant to experience the full spectrum of emotion—not to be consumed by it, but to evolve through it. In attaching ourselves to pain, we sometimes lose fragments of our soul. We forget our sovereignty, our wholeness, and fall into the illusion of lack, limitation, and separation.

A fragmented soul feels incomplete—like something essential is missing. There may be a sense of numbness or disconnection, a quiet apathy that mutes the vibrancy of life. We may feel as though we are merely existing, moving through a dream. Eventually, this dissonance becomes undeniable, and we're forced to confront it. It is in this moment of awakening that healing begins.

The journey of soul retrieval is one of remembrance and reconnection. Through practices such as meditation, self-inquiry, creative expression, and deep inner work, we begin to reintegrate lost parts of ourselves. By nurturing self-compassion, we lay the foundation for true healing.

An **integrated soul** is not perfect, but whole. It is characterized by emotional, mental, and spiritual harmony. It holds self-awareness, a sense of purpose, and the resilience to face life's trials with grace. It embraces virtues such as humility, compassion, and faith, not as ideals, but as ways of being.

In the end, healing the fragmented soul begins with *love*—and the greatest expression of that love is **compassion.**

True compassion holds no judgment. It transcends duality, recognizing that all experiences—light and dark, joy and sorrow—are sacred parts of the whole. Nothing is lesser or greater; everything belongs. Through this lens, we return to alignment with our divine origin, reconnecting with the very reason for our incarnation: to expand consciousness.

> We are the many faces of Source, each a unique reflection of the One. Though we may appear separate, we are eternally interconnected. And through compassion, we remember who we truly are.

Chapter 33

Transforming Love from Emotion to Foundation

Love once flickered, soft and shy,
A fleeting spark beneath the sky.
But now it stands, a silent stone,
Rooted deep, its truth full-grown.

No longer tossed by storm or flame,
It bears the weight, it takes no name.
Beyond the pulse, beyond the thrill,
Love is choice, and love is will.

Not just a feeling we chase and lose,
But sacred ground we daily choose.

Love is often seen as a powerful emotion—a feeling of deep affection, attachment, or desire. We chase it, celebrate it, and mourn its loss. But what if love is far more than something we feel? What if love is not merely emotional, but *foundational*—a core principle of existence, the very essence of who we are?

This shift—from experiencing love as fleeting emotion to embodying it as divine foundation—is not only transformative, it is essential for both personal awakening and collective healing.

Love Beyond Emotion

Culturally, love is portrayed as conditional and reactive. "I love you because…" or "I love you if…" are common mindsets. This makes love fragile—vulnerable to moods, mistakes, and not reciprocated. We become dependent and desperate on external validation for a sense of connection.

True love, however, is not conditional. It isn't dependent on another person's behavior or on how we feel in the moment. Rather than something we fall into or out of, it is something we *become*. Real love doesn't react—it radiates and expands. It is self-generating and rooted in presence.

Divine Love: Unchanging and Eternal

Unlike human love, divine love—*Agape*—is unwavering. It does not ask for anything in return. It sees through flaws and embraces the whole person. This is the love described in sacred texts: the love that mirrors the Creator, the love that defines our divine nature.

When we recognize that we are created in love, from love, for love, we no longer seek it outside ourselves. We realize that love is our natural state and the very essence of who we are.

The Frequency of Love

Science is beginning to support what mystics have long said: love is a high-frequency state of being. The heart's electromagnetic field is 5,000 times stronger than the brain's. Heart-centered emotions like gratitude and compassion create physiological coherence—a state where heart, mind, and body are in harmonious alignment.

Practices like deep breathing, mindfulness, and focusing on uplifting emotions help us access this state of coherence. In it, we are calm, clear, and connected—not only to ourselves but to the energy of love that permeates everything.

Even sound is part of this story. The 528 Hz Solfeggio frequency—sometimes called the "love frequency"—is believed to support healing and inner balance. Whether or not we measure it scientifically, many feel this vibration resonates with something deeply true within them.

Becoming the Frequency

Understanding love as a vibration changes how we engage with it. We stop trying to *get* love, and instead focus on *being* love. Every act of kindness, every moment of stillness, every conscious breath becomes a way to tune in to this higher state.

Love becomes a practice, a posture, a choice. We create from it. We lead with it. We live in alignment with its frequency. When love is our foundation, we stop living in reaction and start living in intention.

Agape: The Sacred Way of Being

The highest form of love—Agape—is selfless and unconditional. It is not naïve or passive, but deeply rooted in truth and wholeness. Agape allows us to love without judgment, to hold compassion even in pain, and to offer grace while still maintaining boundaries.

To love in this way is to reflect the divine. It's to meet life and others not with fear or expectation, but with the fullness of presence and sacred respect.

From Seeking Love to Being Love

This transformation—from emotion to foundation—is the soul's greatest return. We stop asking, "Who will love me?" and start asking, "How can I embody love more fully?"

We remember that love is not something to chase. It is something we are meant to live. In that remembrance, we move from scarcity to sufficiency, from longing to fulfillment.

Conclusion: Love as Our True Nature

To live love as a foundation is to awaken to the truth of our being. It is to see love not as a response to others, but as the very ground we stand on. We become instruments of grace, attuned to the vibration of the Divine.

When love becomes our foundation, it transforms everything—how we see ourselves, how we relate to others, and how we walk through the world. In this state, we no longer just receive love. We *become* love. And in doing so, we fulfill the highest purpose of our existence.

Chapter 34

Quantum Jumping Through the Matrix

Through veils of code and shifting light,
I leap beyond the edge of night.
No doors, no walls, just open space,
A mirrored mind, a timeless place.

I bend the grid with thought alone,
Each thread a path I've always known.
In every choice, a world is spun,
Yet all return to Source as one.

So here I jump, no fear, no strife,
A dreamer dancing into life.

The world we inhabit is not inherently flawed, but rather manipulated, a *false matrix*, disconnected from the organic, divine matrix of the universe. This artificial reality distorts our perceptions, veiling our true essence. It mirrors the Vedantic concept of *Maya*, the grand illusion, which places obstacles on the path to self-realization. These are not accidental, they are deliberate constructs designed to keep us from remembering who we truly are: pure, unconditioned consciousness.

To discover our true purpose and live a life aligned with our highest values, we must transcend this illusory matrix. Escaping it requires inner work—breaking free from societal norms, cultural conditioning, and habitual beliefs that obscure our authentic selves. It is a journey inward, a peeling away of false identities until only the naked truth remains. This awakening reconnects us to our divine nature and births *unity consciousness*, a state where separation dissolves, and the illusion of linear time collapses. In this state, all moments exist simultaneously, there is no past or future, only the eternal *now*.

From a scientific perspective, the concept of consciousness as a quantum phenomenon offers a fascinating parallel. The *quantum mind* theory suggests that classical physics and neuronal activity alone cannot explain consciousness. Instead, quantum mechanics, particularly principles like *entanglement* and *superposition*, may play a role in shaping awareness through nonlocal interactions at sub-cellular levels of the brain. While these ideas remain speculative and unproven, they intersect with the realm of *quantum mysticism*.

Quantum entanglement describes the phenomenon where particles become interlinked across any distance, measuring one immediately affects the other. Superposition allows a quantum entity to exist in multiple states simultaneously, collapsing into a definite state only when observed. These concepts fuel quantum mysticism, which posits that consciousness not only interacts with but also influences reality. The *observer effect*, where observation changes the outcome of a quantum system, is often cited as evidence that consciousness is not passive but creative, that we actively shape the universe through awareness and intention.

Building on this, *quantum jumping* is a metaphorical and sometimes literal practice of shifting one's consciousness from a limited, false reality to a higher, more desired state. It involves cultivating a belief in infinite possibilities, shedding restrictive beliefs, and consciously directing energy toward a new reality. Visualization, emotional alignment, and the intentional harnessing of imagination are key tools. Through focused thought and vibrational alignment, we can tune ourselves to different timelines and potentials, effectively "jumping" from one reality to another.

This transformative process invites us to reclaim our role as conscious co-creators of reality. It is not just a metaphysical theory, but a call to awaken, to live intentionally, imagine vividly, and remember deeply.

In a world shaped by illusions and bound by limiting paradigms, quantum jumping offers a liberating path to reconnection with our divine essence. By transcending the false matrix, embracing unity consciousness, and consciously engaging with the creative power of thought and intention, we align with the greater truth of our being. In doing so, we not only reshape our own reality, we contribute to the awakening of the collective soul, bridging the gap between science, spirituality, and self-realization.

Chapter 35

Soul Trap and the Karmic Wheel

A shimmered light, a whispered plea,
Drawn down through veils of mystery.
The soul descends, forgets its name,
Entwined in birth, in death, in flame.

The karmic wheel begins to spin,
Each deed, each thought, a tethered sin.
Around and round, the lifetimes reel,
A loop of fate none seem to feel.

False gods above, with honeyed lies,
We chase illusions in disguise.
Yet deep within, a truth concealed,
The trap is known, the self unsealed.

Break free, O soul, from dream and bind,
Let silence guide, let stillness find.
For once awakened, none can steal
The light beyond the karmic wheel.

In many Eastern traditions, including Hinduism, Buddhism, and Jainism, **karma** is understood as the law of cause and effect. Our actions, thoughts, and intentions in one life create karmic imprints that shape our future lives and rebirths. This ongoing cycle of birth, death, and rebirth, often called *samsara*, is fueled by karma. Within this framework, the soul is considered to be trapped in this cycle until it attains liberation, *moksha* in Hinduism, *nirvana* in Buddhism.

In Jainism, karma is perceived even more tangibly, as a subtle material substance that clings to the soul, binding it to samsara. Across these belief systems, karma and reincarnation are intrinsically linked: the karma accumulated in one life determines the circumstances of the next, including one's physical form and life conditions.

Karma, then, determines where and how you return. Throughout a lifetime, individuals generate both good and bad karma through their choices and actions, which directly influence their future incarnations. Hindu scriptures identify three types of karma:

- **Sanchita:** accumulated karma from past lives,

- **Prarabdha:** a portion of that karma chosen to be experienced in the current life, and

- **Kriyamana:** karma being created in the present moment.

In Buddhism, the path to freedom from samsara lies in achieving *nirvana*, a state beyond suffering. This is realized through understanding the Four Noble Truths and following the Eightfold Path. Central to this path is overcoming attachment, cultivating compassion, and perceiving reality as it truly is.

Similarly, in Hinduism, while karma cannot be erased, it can be balanced and transformed through righteous living, spiritual discipline, and non-attachment to outcomes. The goal is *moksha,* liberation from the cycle of rebirth, achieved by fulfilling one's *dharma* (sacred duty) without clinging to worldly desires.

According to these belief systems, no matter how many lifetimes it takes, the soul has a clear path to liberation. But what if there are other forces at play beyond our personal karmic actions, forces that actively sustain this cycle? What if samsara is not merely a natural process but part of a greater manipulation, what some refer to as a **soul trap**? If so, who—or what, is orchestrating this?

The "soul trap" theory, though not part of mainstream spirituality, posits that the cycle of rebirth is artificially maintained. Proponents suggest that deceptive entities or a "false light" misguide souls at the moment of death, recycling them into new lives to perpetuate karmic debt and suffering. This theory implies that reincarnation may not be a path of evolution, but rather a spiritual loop created by hidden forces.

This idea intersects with Gnostic teachings. In Gnosticism, **soul traps** and **archons**—ruling entities believed to control the material world—are seen as barriers to spiritual liberation. Archons are depicted as powerful, often malevolent beings that have created a false reality to imprison the soul. The physical world itself is viewed as a kind of cosmic illusion or prison.

Gnosticism holds that the soul's true home is in a higher, divine realm—and that the path to freedom lies in *gnosis* (from the Greek, meaning "knowledge"). This isn't intellectual knowledge, but direct, experiential awareness of divine truth. Gnosis enables the soul to transcend the material world and escape the cycle of reincarnation. Practices such as meditation, contemplation, and inner revelation were ways that ancient Gnostics sought this liberation.

Today, we find ourselves at a pivotal moment. A **collective awakening** is underway. More people than ever are engaging in spiritual exploration beyond traditional religious boundaries. There's a growing interest in turning inward for truth, exploring concepts like consciousness, the unified field, and even quantum principles as keys to transcending the dualistic matrix we live in.

I believe we are now beginning to open ourselves to the universal energy that is guiding this awakening. We are becoming vessels for a new paradigm, one that resonates with our divine essence and aligns us with a higher frequency of truth and liberation.

Four Noble Paths in Buddism:

1. **The Truth of Suffering (Dukkha):** This truth recognizes that life is characterized by suffering, dissatisfaction, and unsatisfactoriness. It's not just physical pain, but also mental and emotional distress, as well as the general unsatisfying nature of human existence.

2. **The Truth of the Origin of Suffering (Samudaya):** This truth identifies the root cause of suffering as craving, attachment, and ignorance. It's the clinging to things, desires, and the belief in a self that leads to suffering.

3. **The Truth of the Cessation of Suffering (Nirodha):** _This truth states that suffering can be overcome and extinguished by eliminating the causes of suffering. It speaks of <u>Nirvana</u>, a state of liberation where there is no more craving or attachment.

4. **The Truth of the Path (Magga):** This truth outlines the <u>Eightfold Path</u>, a practical guide to achieving enlightenment and ending suffering. The Eightfold Path involves ethical conduct, mental discipline, and wisdom.

Eightfold Path:

1. Right Understanding (Samma Ditthi): A clear understanding of the Four Noble Truths, which are the foundation of Buddhist teachings. This includes understanding the nature of suffering, its cause, the path to its end, and the path that leads to the end of suffering.

2. Right Thought (Samma Sankappa): Having positive, wholesome intentions and thoughts that are free from greed, hatred, and harmful intentions.

3. Right Speech (Samma Vaca): Abstaining from lying, gossip, harsh language, and idle chatter.

4. Right Action (Samma Kammanta): Avoiding harmful actions like killing, stealing, and sexual misconduct.

5. Right Livelihood (Samma Ajiva): Earning a living through honest and ethical means, avoiding occupations that involve harming others.

6. Right Effort (Samma Vayama): Cultivating positive mental states and abandoning negative ones, striving to maintain wholesome states of mind.

7. Right Mindfulness (Samma Sati): Being fully aware of the present moment, paying attention to the body, feelings, mind, and mental qualities.

8. Right Concentration (Samma Samadhi): Developing the ability to focus the mind and cultivate mental stability, leading to deeper meditative states.

Chapter 36

Patience: Waiting for Divine Timing

In silence deep, the soul must wait,
Not rushing fate, nor tempting it.
For seeds once sown must find their hour,
To bloom with grace in heaven's power.

What's meant to be will come to stay,
Not one breath early, nor delay.
So trust the flow, release control—
Divine timing knows the goal.

In the fast-paced world we live in today, everything seems to happen in the blink of an eye. We are constantly multitasking, striving to accomplish multiple goals at once, driven by a culture of productivity and competition. Rapid technological advancements—such as high-speed internet, 5G connectivity, and AI innovation—have intensified this momentum, reinforcing the expectation of instant gratification. But in the midst of this relentless pursuit, one must ask: *Are we truly designed to keep up with such speed? Is this race in* alignment with the natural rhythm of our bodies and souls?

Though we may believe we can match this pace, the limitations of our human form inevitably surface. Fatigue, burnout, and emotional collapse remind us that we are not machines. When we cannot keep up, disappointment creeps in, leading to discouragement and a sense of failure. This state of imbalance affects our psyche, often leaving us feeling hopeless and disconnected.

When we allow these external forces to dictate our internal rhythms, we hinder the natural unfolding of our lives. Blessings and experiences meant to come into our lives when we are fully prepared may arrive prematurely or never at all. Just as a child prematurely opens a cocoon in hopes of seeing a butterfly, only to harm its transformation, we too damage the beauty of life when we force outcomes before their time. Life is meant to be lived in the present—not in regrets of the past or the projections of the future.

Patience is not just a virtue; it is a spiritual necessity. It helps us remain grounded in the present moment and aligned with our soul's path. Without patience, we risk veering off course, chasing timelines that may not be meant for us, and losing sight of our higher purpose. This detour doesn't just affect us—it may also impact the lives and destinies of others we are meant to journey with or co-create alongside.

At its core, patience is about trust—trust in a higher power, in divine timing, and in the wisdom of our own inner guidance. It means enduring challenges with grace, knowing there is a sacred order to life's unfolding. It is a conscious alignment with the divine self, allowing life to evolve organically rather than being manipulated by ego or fear.

Across spiritual traditions, patience is seen as a gateway to inner peace and deeper faith. It cultivates resilience, humility, and compassion—for ourselves and for others. It is not a passive state of waiting but an active surrender, a disciplined awareness that the right moment will come. In this way, patience becomes a form of wisdom—one that honors timing as sacred rather than something to control.

To practice patience is to embrace the mystery of life. It is to slow down, tune into the present, and trust that delays are not denials but divine preparation. Waiting becomes a sacred space for growth, refinement, and readiness.

Ultimately, "Patience: Waiting for Divine Timing" is an invitation to relinquish control and surrender to the rhythm of the universe. It reminds us that what is meant for us will not pass us by—so long as we are willing to trust, wait, and walk in faith. In patience, we discover the beauty of perfect timing.

Chapter 37

Perspective, Perspective, Perspective

The lens through which we choose to see
Can shackle minds or set them free.
A shift in view, a softened gaze,
Turns darkest nights to golden days.

The mountain high, the valley low—
Each holds a truth we ought to know.
What once was curse may be a gift,
If only we allow the shift.

So pause, reflect, and dare to find
The wisdom in a changed mind's light.
Perspective, whispered thrice, will be
The path from pain to clarity.

From the mountaintop, the valley appears still and serene, while from the depths of the valley, the mountaintop seems distant and unreachable. Both views are valid. Both are true. Yet neither tells the whole story. Such is the nature of perspective.

In our journey through life—across the terrain of thoughts, emotions, experiences, and awakenings—what we see and believe is shaped less by what is actually in front of us and more by the lens through which we view it. Our beliefs, traumas, cultural conditioning, desires, fears, and aspirations all color the way we perceive the world. This is why the same event can uplift one person and devastate another. This is why two people can experience the same relationship, yet walk away with radically different narratives. It's all a matter of *perspective, perspective, perspective.*

The Illusion of Absoluteness

We often fall prey to the illusion that our view is *the* truth. That how we interpret an event is how it inherently is. But truth, in its purest spiritual form, is not confined to singular experiences or finite interpretations. It is vast, multifaceted, and layered beyond human comprehension. Just as a prism splits light into many colors, reality reveals different aspects depending on the angle of observation.

To awaken spiritually is to transcend this illusion of absoluteness and begin to see that our perceptions are not fixed realities, but reflections of our inner states. A cloudy mind sees storms where there are none; a peaceful heart sees the light even in the darkest corners.

Many of us live trapped in our own perspectives without realizing it. We view others through the lens of our wounds. We judge situations based on past pain or future fear. We resist change because we are looking at it through the lens of loss rather than potential. Every step on the spiritual path is an invitation to step back from the lens, to expand the field of vision, and to ask, "What else could this mean?"

Shifting from Victimhood to Empowerment

Consider this: two individuals lose their jobs. One spirals into despair, consumed by unworthiness and fear. The other sees it as a sign to pursue a deeper calling, finally free to walk the path of purpose they once feared to tread. Same event. Different perspective.

The first individual may ask, "Why is life so unfair to me?" while the second might declare, "Life is redirecting me toward something greater." One sinks, the other soars—not because of circumstance, but because of perception.

The shift from victimhood to empowerment begins when we realize that we are not helpless recipients of life's events, but co-creators of meaning. We may not control everything that happens to us, but we can always choose how we interpret and respond. This is not spiritual bypassing—it's spiritual alchemy. The art of transmuting pain into purpose, loss into liberation, and endings into new beginnings.

Every experience is a mirror reflecting something back to us. Sometimes it shows our strength. Other times, it reveals areas still governed by fear, ego, or illusion. To see clearly, we must clean the mirror. And that cleansing begins with humility—the humility to accept that our view may be limited, and the willingness to look again with fresh eyes.

The Role of Ego in Perspective

The ego thrives on certainty. It wants to be right. It clings to stories that affirm its sense of identity. But the soul craves expansion. It longs for understanding that goes beyond the self. Where the ego says, "This is how it is," the soul asks, "What more can be revealed here?"

The ego filters everything through a binary lens: good or bad, success or failure, friend or foe. But the soul sees the paradox in all things. It sees that light and shadow dance together. That a heartbreak can open the heart wider. That a moment of humiliation can birth humility and grace.

To shift perspective, we must loosen the ego's grip. This doesn't mean abandoning the ego—it serves its purpose in navigating the human world—but it does mean stepping into the observer role. To ask ourselves: "Is this the only way to see this situation? What would my higher self perceive here?"

This question is powerful because it invites us into the multidimensionality of truth. It disrupts the autopilot of judgment and reactive emotion. It creates space for compassion, for stillness, for insight. In this space, miracles can unfold—not because the outer situation changes, but because we do.

Spiritual Growth Through Perspective

Spiritual maturity is often less about accumulating knowledge and more about refining perspective. A child sees a rainstorm as a ruined day; a farmer sees it as a blessing. A traveler may curse a delayed flight; a mystic may see it as divine protection. The same event, again, filtered through different lenses.

When we begin to see life as happening *for* us rather than *to* us, a profound shift occurs. We realize that even the most painful chapters have encoded wisdom. That adversity is not punishment, but invitation. That challenges stretch the soul's capacity to love, to endure, to rise.

This doesn't mean we celebrate suffering or bypass grief. It means we learn to hold both pain and perspective. To allow sorrow to deepen us without defining us. To trust that every step, even the detour, is part of a greater unfolding.

Perspective teaches patience. What feels like a failure today may reveal itself as a redirection in a year. What feels like betrayal now may one day be seen as liberation. Time often shifts perspective more than reason can. This is why spiritual reflection requires not just intellect, but surrender.

Seeing Others Through the Eyes of Compassion

One of the most powerful spiritual practices is learning to see others through new eyes. We are quick to judge, quick to categorize. But what if we paused and asked, "What pain shaped this person's behavior? What fear might they be acting from? What unmet need lies beneath their mask?"

This shift in perspective softens us. It replaces condemnation with curiosity, resentment with compassion. It allows us to forgive—not because what happened was okay, but because we recognize the human behind the act.

Seeing others with new eyes also means letting go of the need to be understood and leaning into the desire to understand. It means choosing empathy over ego, connection over correctness. This is not weakness—it is spiritual strength.

When we view relationships through the lens of soul growth rather than emotional gratification, we stop labeling people as right or wrong, good or bad. Instead, we ask, "What lesson is this soul contract teaching me? What part of me is being mirrored back for healing?"

Perspective becomes a portal to deeper love.

Universal Perspective: The Divine Lens

At the highest level, perspective is about alignment with divine vision. Imagine seeing the world through the eyes of God—where every being is sacred, every path is honored, and every moment is purposeful. Where no soul is lesser, no journey wasted. Where love is the ground of all being.

This is the vision mystics, sages, and awakened beings have sought to embody. Not because they transcended suffering, but because they embraced it with clarity and love. They saw the oneness beneath separation. They understood that all perspectives are but fragments of an infinite truth.

To cultivate this divine perspective is to awaken the third eye—not just as a mystical symbol, but as the inner vision that sees beyond the veil. It means perceiving energy over appearances, essence over ego, eternal over temporary.

In this state, judgment dissolves. Grievances lose their grip. Life becomes a sacred play, and each actor is seen as a fellow traveler—learning, stumbling, growing, remembering.

Practical Tools to Cultivate Perspective

1. **Pause and Breathe**

In the moment of emotional reactivity, take a breath. Pause. Ask yourself, "What else could be true here?" This small act creates space for a shift.

2. **Journaling from Multiple Angles**

When reflecting on a difficult situation, write about it from three perspectives: yours, the other person's, and your higher self's. This exercise unveils hidden truths.

3. **Gratitude for the Challenge**

List three things you learned or gained from a painful experience. Even if it's hard, this helps reframe the event as a teacher rather than a tormentor.

4. **Mirror Work**

Look into your own eyes in a mirror and affirm, "I am willing to see this differently." This practice softens the ego and opens the heart.

5. **Conscious Conversations**

When in conflict, strive to listen deeply. Say, "Help me understand your perspective." This invites connection rather than defense.

The Sacred Repetition

Why say "Perspective" three times?

Because it takes repetition to remember. It takes layers of unlearning and re-seeing to peel away the illusion. We must be reminded again and again:

- That our current viewpoint is not the only one.
- That we can change our minds and expand our hearts.

- That divine truth is vaster than our temporary understanding.

Perspective, perspective, perspective—a sacred chant. A spiritual mantra. A guiding star on the path of awakening.

Conclusion: The Gift of New Vision

As we journey through life, we are constantly being offered new lenses—through heartbreak and joy, through loss and discovery. Each shift in perspective is a small death of ego and a birth of soul.

In the end, awakening is not about escaping the world but seeing it with new eyes. Eyes that behold the divine in the mundane. Eyes that look at the same sky and see not just clouds, but infinite possibility.

May we walk gently, question deeply, and see clearly. May we remember that nothing is ever as it seems—and that everything is sacred, when seen through the eyes of the soul.

Perspective, perspective, perspective.

The key to wisdom.
The seed of peace.
The doorway to the Divine.

Chapter 38

Be the Change You Wish to See in the World

A single spark can light the flame,
A whispered truth can shift the game.
Don't wait for others to begin—
The change you seek must grow within.
With open heart and steady hand,
Take one small step, then boldly stand.
For when you lead with soul and grace,
You help transform the human race.

Many of us carry a persistent desire for perfection—an urge to earn the highest score, avoid mistakes, and live flawlessly. It's almost instinctive for us as human beings to want more, to be more, and to do more. Yet, in our relentless pursuit of idealism, we often overlook a fundamental truth: we live in an imperfect world. So why do we expect ourselves to be any different?

Ironically, it is our very imperfections—and our willingness to embrace them—that pave the way to authentic happiness. We all have faults. We've made mistakes, we have habits we wish to break, and we'll undoubtedly stumble again. But rather than allowing these flaws to define us or burying ourselves in self-doubt, we can choose a different path: one that acknowledges our humanity while leaning into our strengths.

Too often, people are weighed down by internalized beliefs like "I'm not good enough" or "I'm not doing enough." These thoughts become mental barriers that cloud our potential. But when we shift our focus—when we choose to see our strengths, nurture our gifts, and believe in our capacity to grow—our entire outlook transforms. This mindset shift not only elevates our own lives but can influence others in profound ways.

The famous quote, "Be the change that you wish to see in the world," often attributed to Mahatma Gandhi, captures this beautifully. While the wording may not be found verbatim in his writings, the essence of the message is unmistakably aligned with his teachings: true change starts from within.

Personal transformation is a powerful force. When we take responsibility for our inner growth, it naturally extends outward—affecting our families, our communities, and even the world. By cultivating qualities like self-awareness, compassion, emotional intelligence, and resilience, we become catalysts for broader transformation.

As we grow, we begin to show up differently—in our relationships, our careers, and our contributions to society. We become better listeners, more empathetic leaders, and more engaged citizens. Our personal shifts, though subtle at times, can spark collective waves of change. A single act of kindness, a word of encouragement, or a choice rooted in awareness can uplift another—and that influence can ripple across generations.

In a world that often feels chaotic and divided, it is tempting to wait for someone else to fix things. But the most meaningful revolutions begin not in government halls or public stages—they begin in the quiet resolve of the human heart. Each time we choose growth over comfort, love over fear, and purpose over passivity, we shape a better world.

So let us remember: we are not powerless. We are the seeds of the change we long to see. And when we choose to embody that change—day by day, moment by moment—we help light the way for others to follow. In transforming ourselves, we become the very solution the world is waiting for.

Chapter 39

See the Invisible: Believe in the Impossible

Faith is not sight, yet clear as day,
A whisper within that lights the way.
It sees beyond what eyes reveal,
And trusts in truths the soul can feel.

Not bound to form, nor time, nor place,
It walks with strength, it moves with grace.
Aligned with purpose, calm and still,
It flows in tune with higher will.

Though storms may rise and plans may fall,
The faithful heart will heed the call.
For in the void, where doubts may dwell,
The light of trust begins to swell.

So close your eyes, and you shall see—
The unseen path to what can be.
Believe beyond what minds construe,
The impossible lives inside of you.

Faith is often defined as a strong belief or trust in something, especially in the absence of concrete proof. At its core, faith involves deep conviction, unwavering confidence, and complete trust—whether in a person, principle, or higher power. Within a religious context, faith typically means belief in God, in divine promises, and in spiritual truths that surpass physical evidence.

Yet faith transcends mere belief. It is an inner conviction that shapes thought, inspires action, and sustains hope even in the darkest hours. It is not passive; rather, it calls us to live in accordance with what we believe, turning invisible truths into visible acts.

But what if the source of that faith is not external, but internal? What if faith is less about worshiping something outside of ourselves and more about aligning with a deeper, higher aspect of who we truly are—a divine self that perceives life from a vantage beyond ego and illusion? In this light, faith becomes alignment. It is the synchronization of our human actions with divine will—a unity of belief and behavior anchored in inner knowing.

Such alignment requires more than intellectual agreement; it demands full surrender. To live in this kind of faith is to trust wholly in the process, to release control over outcomes, and to believe without doubt in the benevolence of the unfolding journey. Even when life does not go according to our plans, we rest in the assurance that everything will ultimately align for the highest good—no matter how long it may take. Surrender releases resistance. In surrender, we enter flow. And in flow, we are no longer stuck; instead, we dance with life's impermanence and remain open to transformation.

Science now confirms what mystics have long known: faith transforms the mind. Through the phenomenon of neuroplasticity—the brain's ability to rewire itself—consistent spiritual practice reshapes our inner world. Practices such as meditation, prayer, and mindfulness enhance concentration, regulate emotion, and strengthen pathways associated with peace, empathy, and resilience. They calm the fear-driven centers of the brain and activate those responsible for joy and connection. Belief, particularly when rooted in love and trust, initiates the release of neurochemicals that nourish our mental and emotional well-being.

Moreover, faith offers a framework for navigating adversity. It gives meaning to suffering and fosters compassion, gratitude, and service. These values are not just noble—they are neurologically beneficial. They cultivate a heart-brain coherence that supports both personal healing and social harmony.

The phrase *"See the invisible, believe in the impossible,"* often attributed to Corrie ten Boom—a Dutch Christian evangelist and Holocaust survivor—beautifully captures this essence. Her faith empowered her to perceive beyond her circumstances and hold fast to possibilities others could not see. This is the nature of tested faith: it looks beyond appearances, trusts what is yet unseen, and dares to hope where logic says there is none.

When we align with our inner divinity—our source of true faith—we embody courage, compassion, and unwavering purpose. Our lives become a living testimony of trust in something greater than ourselves. This alignment doesn't just guide us through life's storms; it transforms us from within.

Closing Reflection:

To *see the invisible* is to look with spiritual eyes. To *believe in the impossible* is to trust the unseen potential of the soul. When we harmonize our inner truth with divine will, faith ceases to be a distant hope and becomes a living force. In this sacred alignment, miracles are not merely possible—they are inevitable.

Chapter 40

Heart: The Center of Our Being

Within the chest, a beacon glows,
Where silent truth and feeling flows.
Not just a pulse, but soul's own flame,
A sacred space with love as name.

It holds our joy, our deepest ache,
The vows we keep, the paths we take.
It hums with grace, it sings with pain—
Yet always calls us home again.

Through heart we feel, through heart we know,
The light within, the soul's soft glow.
A bridge to Source, both near and far—
The heart reveals just who we are

The heart has long been regarded as more than just a vital organ—it is the symbolic center of our inner life, encompassing thought, emotion, intention, and desire. It is often called the wellspring of life, where love, joy, compassion, and even fear and anger emerge. Across cultures and spiritual traditions, the heart is seen not only as the seat of deep emotion but as a sacred space where the soul meets the divine.

In spiritual frameworks, the heart is a place of revelation and intuitive knowing. It is believed to hold wisdom that transcends logic, offering insights that arise from within rather than from external reasoning. This intuitive function is complemented by the heart's physical capabilities. Studies suggest that the heart can influence the brain's self-regulation, highlighting a connection between emotion, cognition, and physiological well-being.

Psychologically, the heart represents our need for nurturing relationships and meaningful connection. When our emotional center is secure and supported, we cultivate qualities such as trust, belonging, and personal integrity. A pure heart—one aligned in thought, word, and action—is often considered the hallmark of spiritual maturity and inner harmony.

From a scientific perspective, the heart generates a powerful electromagnetic field that extends several feet beyond the body. This field is not a passive phenomenon—it actively communicates information both within and beyond the body. Emotions significantly affect this field: positive states like love and gratitude generate coherent, harmonious rhythms, while stress and anger create disordered patterns. This coherence, or lack thereof, influences not only our own health and emotional balance but also our interactions with others.

Some research suggests that this energetic field contributes to a subtle but profound form of interconnectedness. Emotions may influence others through shared energy fields, even across great distances. In this sense, the heart becomes an instrument of energetic communication, bonding us through unseen yet felt frequencies.

Practices like meditation, mindfulness, and gratitude have been shown to help cultivate heart coherence. These practices help us shift from reactive states to a more grounded, compassionate way of being. Over time, such practices can train the heart to generate more beneficial rhythms, enhancing both emotional well-being and spiritual alignment.

There are also fascinating ideas linking the human heart to the Earth's natural electromagnetic frequency, known as the Schumann Resonance. While not conclusively proven, some evidence suggests that humans may respond to this global frequency, with potential effects on brainwaves, hormonal balance, and general well-being. This connection hints at a subtle synchrony between human life and the planet, reinforcing the idea of an intimate link between the physical and spiritual dimensions of our existence.

Across spiritual traditions, the heart is revered as the dwelling place of divine presence and the source of inner light. In **Hinduism**, it is considered the abode of the Lord and the center of consciousness and devotion. In **Judaism**, the heart holds both emotion and wisdom, essential for spiritual understanding. In **Christianity**, the heart and mind are seen as deeply interconnected, shaping one's spiritual journey and relationship with God.

Ultimately, the heart is not only a physical organ or metaphorical symbol, it is the bridge between our human experience and our divine essence. It is through the heart that we feel connected to others, to the Earth, and to the sacred. In its purity, the heart becomes the compass of the soul, guiding us with empathy, intuition, and the language of love.

Concluding Perspective:

In a world often governed by intellect, speed, and external validation, the heart invites us to slow down and listen inward. It reminds us that true wisdom lies not in information, but in understanding, not in reaction, but in resonance. To live from the heart is to live in alignment, with ourselves, with one another, and with the divine flow of life. It is to embrace the sacred space within us that pulses with compassion, clarity, and connection.

When we tune into the heart, we awaken a universal language—one that speaks not in words, but in presence. Here, we discover that the heart is not just the center of our being, it is the gateway to all that is.

Compassion: The Soul's Embrace

Compassion blooms, a sacred flame,
Beyond mere sorrow, beyond just name.
Not only feeling what others feel—
But reaching out with hands to heal.

For family, we soften with care,
For friends, our empathy we share.
Even strangers, passing by,
Deserve the kindness we supply.

Yet deeper still, the truest art—
Is showing compassion to our own heart.
When shadows rise and harsh thoughts scream,
Self-love becomes the healing stream.

To be as kind as we would be
To a friend in pain or misery.
To know we're flawed, but not alone—
Each wound a seed that we've outgrown.

With mindfulness, we gently see
The storms within, yet choose to be.
To hold our hearts without disdain,
And walk ourselves through inner pain.

But oh, the irony runs deep—
We judge ourselves, our wounds we keep.
Shaped by voices from the past,
We wear a mask, a spell long cast.

The hurts we hide, the trust once burned,
The love denied, the hope unlearned.
These fragments speak in subtle tones,
Our silent traumas carved in stone.

We are actors on a mystic stage,
Directed by unconscious rage.
Who writes this play? Who casts the roles?
Whose grip still clutches at our souls?

In lifetimes past, we've played the part—
Of victim lost and broken heart.
But still the spark of truth remains—
We are not bound by fear or chains.

For we are light, Divine expressed,
In human form, put to the test.
To feel it all—both joy and ache—
Is how our sleeping souls awake.

A fractured soul feels dull and bare,
Like drifting mist in stagnant air.
But deep inside, the longing calls—

To gather what was lost to fall.

The path of wholeness winds within,
Through quiet thought and sacred skin.
Through tears that flow, through art and prayer,
We stitch the self with loving care.

An integrated soul will shine—
Not flawless, but in true design.
At peace with past, with purpose clear,
A steady light that others near.

So let us love the self we hide,
With open arms and gentler eyes.
No part too dark, no wound too deep—
The soul remembers what it seeks.

Compassion holds no sword or scale,
It sees no lesser, no more frail.
It lifts the veil from 'right' and 'wrong',
And sings the truth through Spirit's song.

For we are One, though many seem—
Each soul a thread in Heaven's dream.
And through compassion, pure and wise,
We see ourselves in others' eyes.

About the Author

Arwin Valencia, MD, based in Orange County, California, is a board-certified pediatrician specializing in Neonatology and Perinatology. He completed his medical degree at the University of Santo Tomas, pediatrics residency at Richmond University Medical Center, and fellowship in Neonatal-Perinatal Medicine at the University of California, Irvine.

Dr. Valencia has authored and co-authored numerous peer-reviewed publications on neonatal health, with notable research on oxidative stress, the gut microbiome, necrotizing enterocolitis (NEC), and the effects of corticosteroids on growth and neurodevelopment. His work spans both clinical and translational research, offering insights into conditions such as patent ductus arteriosus and oxygen-induced injury in preterm infants. His publications are well-cited, reflecting his active engagement with the neonatal scientific community.

In addition to his academic contributions, Dr. Valencia serves in leadership roles within the Pediatrix Medical Group, helping to direct neonatal intensive care across multiple hospitals. His work bridges compassionate clinical care with evidence-based innovation, embodying a lifelong commitment to advancing newborn health.

Beyond the clinical setting, Dr. Valencia is a seeker of deeper truths and a passionate advocate of holistic healing. Rooted in both scientific inquiry and spiritual insight, his work bridges medicine and metaphysics, blending modern healthcare with ancient wisdom. He believes that true healing arises from the integration of body, mind, and soul, and that self-awareness is central to compassionate care and conscious living. Through his writings, he invites others on a soulful journey of remembering, of rediscovering the divine essence within each of us.

There is a life force within
your soul, seek that life.
There is a gem in the
mountain of your body,
seek that mine.
O traveller, if you are in search
of that, don't look outside,
look inside yourself and seek that.

Rumi

www.ingramcontent.com/pod-product-compliance
Lightning Source LLC
LaVergne TN
LVHW011419080426
835512LV00005B/141